JOHN DEERE
Collectibles

Brenda Kruse

MBI Publishing Company

Dedication
This book is dedicated to "John Deere Jim" and anyone else who "bleeds green."

First published in 2001 by MBI Publishing Company, Galtier Plaza, Suite 200, 380 Jackson Street, St. Paul, MN 55101-3885 USA

MBI Publishing Company books are also available at discounts in bulk quantity for industrial or sales-promotional use. For details write to Special Sales Manager at Motorbooks International Wholesalers & Distributors, Galtier Plaza, Suite 200, 380 Jackson Street, St. Paul, MN 55101-3885 USA.

Library of Congress Cataloging-in-Publication Data
Kruse, Brenda.
    John Deere collectibles / Brenda Kruse.
        p. cm.
    Includes index.
    ISBN 0-7603-0830-6 (hc. : alk. paper)
    1. John Deere tractors–Collectibles–Catalogs. I. Title.

TL233.6.J64 K78 2001
629.225'2'075–dc21

On the front cover: Although John Deere collectibles range from being cheap and cheesy to popular and pricey, any memorabilia associated with Deere & company is highly sought-after by today's collectors. Illustrating this range, items on the cover show that there are exciting collectibles for anyone.

The walking cultivator wrench, Champion spark plug (in its box), oil can with spout (Part No. JD91) and literature for the Model D, General-Purpose Tractors and Velie automobiles were useful around the farm or dealership.

Items such as the Westclox alarm clock, oil can bank, mailbox bank, celluloid tape measure, change tray, thermometer, clothes brush, desk mirror, pocket knife, needle case, lighter and match safe were handy around the house.

Collectors also value promotional trinkets such as the belt buckle, necklace, factory badge, flag pin, watch fobs, and the Ertl scale-model toy tractor and plow by Eska-Carter. *Nick Cedar*

On the frontispiece: The word "Deere" stamped on anything makes it collectible. These wrenches are identified by parts numbers, which associate the tool with a particular piece of equipment and time period. *Nick Cedar*

On the title page: Collectors can choose from a smorgasboard of John Deere memorabilia—pens, pins, and plows are just a few of the "unique antiques" on the market today. Items shown include a book titled *The Operation, Care, and Repair of Farm Machinery* (28th edition), a straw children's hat bearing the 1950 logo, a "Leaping Lager Team Deere Beer" bottle, an anvil paperweight on a wood base, a 10-inch replica of a walking plow, a plastic dual salt-pepper shaker with a Minnesota dealer imprint, 150th anniversary matchbox, Velie/Deere letter opener, a John Deere Plow Co. Kansas City clutch pin (for saddles, collars, and harness), an employee service award money clip, an Oil can charm, a pearled ballpoint pen with the Studebaker logo, a Kemp & Burpee manure spreader spinner fob, a Waterloo Boy colored button, and a John Deere Tractor Co. bullet lighter. *Nick Cedar*

On the back cover: From rusty wrenches to cast-iron seats, collecting parts and pieces of equipment is just one aspect of the market for John Deere memorabilia. Items shown include a "Power" foldout poster (from Model D tractor literature), a toolbox lid with the 1937 trademark logo, a green oil can with spout (Part No. JD 93), a Velie Motors Corporation hubcap, 1996 pewter Christmas ornament, a belt buckle with epoxy swirl inset, a Deere Mansur Co. wrench (A523), an iridescent centennial marble with base, a two-cylinder tractor matchbook, a plastic tape measure with Moline dealer imprint, a Velie Wrought-Iron Vehicles needlecase, a Van Brunt Manufacturing employee badge, and a bullet pencil on keychain with an Iowa dealer imprint. *Nick Cedar*

Edited by John Adams-Graf
Designed by Dan Perry

Printed in China

CONTENTS

ACKNOWLEDGMENTS

In my quest to create this book, I've been blessed with the good fortune of meeting many incredible individuals whose roles in making this dream a reality I must formally acknowledge.

First and foremost, I appreciate the assistance of the collectors whose prized possessions are featured within these pages—Dale Lenz, Dean Stump, and Marvin Benson. I value their knowledge and insight, as well as their wonderful sense of humor. I also respect their passion for this hobby. They gave generously of their time, trusted me with their treasures, and calmly answered a barrage of questions. While we started out as strangers, we quickly became friends . . . forever bonded by the Great Green.

Another collector deserves special recognition for his effort—my father-in-law Jim Kruse actually hatched the idea to write a book on this topic several years ago. His interest in the hobby was directly responsible for the creation of this book.

A big thank-you to Kurt Aumann, whose knowledge of the industry as a collector and an auctioneer added a special touch. I also wish to thank Les Stegh, Deere & Company archivist, for his efforts in adding dates and details, as well as giving me the opportunity to photograph the very special items in the Archive collection. A warm thanks also goes to Jesse Quinones, whose spirited stories enlightened my view of Deere & Company's history.

To my photographers for sharing their talents by capturing the bits and pieces of John Deere history—Nick Cedar, Denny Eilers, and Michelle Schueder— I applaud your patience when I insisted on getting "just one more shot" of another trinket or treasure.

Thanks to the hundreds of other collectors scattered across the country who offered information that helped fill in the blanks or shared hopeful words to let me know my hard work would be rewarded with grateful readers.

Cheers to my friends and family who helped proofread the manuscript and listened to my rants and raves about the latest developments. Thank you to my clients who knowingly or unknowingly granted me the time and attention needed to accomplish something of this magnitude. And to my Mac G3 computer, which faithfully put in long hours as my partner in this project.

A big hug to my parents, Steve and Ronda Ebel, who raised me to love the smell of the dirt and gave me my first experience with green equipment. They helped develop and nurture my love of the land and encouraged my writing career from day one. I admire them for their hard work and sacrifices, and I respect their dedicated decision to farm.

And last but certainly not least—I want to thank my husband, Korey, who also got a daily dose of Deere from my updates and escapades. His belief that I could do it helped motivate me when this labor of love nearly overwhelmed me. His reminder that "it's only an overview" became my mantra lest I become consumed in my attempt to unearth every single piece of memorabilia and its detailed history. I owe you for your support as my spouse, best friend, and ever-encouraging editor!

If, by chance, I've left anyone out . . . as we say in New Mexico, ¡muchas gracias!

INTRODUCTION

Since John Deere forged his first plowshare in 1837, the Deere brand of farm equipment has played a significant role in developing agriculture as it exists today. In farming, the legacy of a livelihood is passed on from generation to generation; the land, the farmhouse, the tractors, and other equipment are all part of the package. The same can be said for a corporation founded by a family. Today, that famous company embarks on a new generation.

The vast history of Deere & Company spans more than 160 years—surviving a long list of economic, political, environmental, and international threats. The company persevered through many major wars and several significant economic downturns, such as the Great Depression of the 1930s and the Farm Crisis of the 1980s. From growing government regulations to changing farmer preferences abroad, Deere's global business weathered economical instability, import-export restrictions, and labor unrest, as well as communication challenges due to differences in customs and language.

As the fourth-oldest corporation in America, Deere & Company is characterized by industry innovation, lasting leadership, and engineering excellence. A recent consolidation of rival agricultural equipment manufacturers left Deere & Company the only such full-line manufacturer to avoid an acquisition or merger into another entity. As a tribute to this accomplishment, Wayne Broehl's words from his 1984 book, *John Deere's Company: A History of Deere & Company and its Times*, still hold true today:

Only a small number of American businesses today have had a life extending back to a period before the Civil War. Those that do, in the main, are successful businesses. Those that did not survive—weakened by recurring business cycles, changing tastes, or inept leadership—were taken over, liquidated, or forced into bankruptcy. Many more famous names of yesteryear were obliterated in mergers and other corporate vicissitudes.

While Deere's claim to fame rests with its long green line of farm equipment, John Deere also put its name on a family of construction equipment, plus lawn and garden machines. What might surprise even the seasoned collector is the long list of other manufacturing ventures that hold a place in Deere & Company's storied history: buggies, wagons, saddles, automobiles, airplanes, bicycles, fertilizer—even silos!

No matter what the product, the name John Deere has always been associated with quality equipment. This dedication came directly from its founder, who once said, "I will never put my name on a plow which does not have in it the best that is in me." With the familiar icons of the plow, the leaping deer, and the green-and-yellow paint, Deere & Company built a brand that enjoys worldwide recognition and respect. Today, collectors of John Deere memorabilia carry on the company's fame by preserving bits and pieces of its history.

CHAPTER 1

Bleeding Green:
A Collectors' Phenomenon

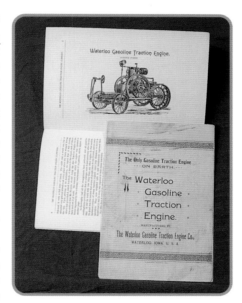

The name John Deere conjures up the sights, sounds, and smells of the farm. Images of bright green tractors working in the field come quickly to mind. The distinctive popping sounds of two-cylinder engines echo with a familiar ring in the ear. It's easy to recall the sweet fragrance of fresh-cut hay as well as the pungent odor of hog manure. The farm is a place that excites the senses and encourages a healthy dose of nostalgia for many people.

Nostalgia is a wistful or sentimental longing for places, things, acquaintances, or conditions belonging to the past. It certainly describes the way collectors feel connected to John Deere. This powerful bond is understandable for those raised in a rural lifestyle. Others did not grow up on an agricultural acre, but have fond memories of summer visits to grandpa's farm.

The hobby of collecting is nothing new, although the growing emphasis on John Deere is a relatively recent occurrence. Seasoned collectors estimate the market for both antique equipment and related memorabilia has almost doubled in the past decade. No one can pinpoint the reason for this intense interest in antique agriculture. Sociologists may be tempted to credit—or blame—the Baby Boom generation, citing its members' tendency to surround themselves with nostalgia as they age.

Regardless of who drives the movement, the fact is, John Deere collecting is experiencing an impressive growth spurt. Who are the people involved in this craze? Collectors come in all sizes and shapes, but in just one color—John Deere Green. As you might expect, there is no such thing as a "typical" John Deere collector. These individuals are scattered across the country . . . and even the globe.

Who Bleeds Green?

John Deere collectors may be retired farmers or still actively engaged in making a living from agriculture. They may be employees of the Deere & Company or its factories and dealerships. Or they may work in a related business such as publishing, marketing, or broadcasting. Some collectors may have no obvious connection to John Deere or agriculture, but feel a special affinity for the brand as a result of family influence. For example,

When it comes to collecting John Deere, the possibilities are seemingly unlimited. A long history coupled with many mergers and product diversifications have left behind thousands of Deere-associated items for enthusiasts to collect. The center panel of this very colorful tri-fold brochure promotes garden tools from Deere & Mansur. *Nick Cedar*

Above: Engineering pioneer John Froelich built the first tractor in 1892. The Waterloo Gasoline Traction Engine Company of Waterloo, Iowa touted this "gasoline traction engine" as the only one on earth. Unfortunately, Froelich's invention didn't instantly propel the company to fame and fortune. The stationary engine line kept the company afloat while Froelich experimented. By 1911, the company built the first official Waterloo Boy design, which John Deere eventually absorbed into its product line in 1918. With 12 pages of black text and sketched images, this rare piece of tractor history recently sold for $1,700 at an auction in the Midwest. *Brenda Kruse*

A sinister hat-wearing skull that graced the back page of the 1899 product catalog from the John Deere Plow Company of Kansas City boasted, "We Laugh at Competition." *Brenda Kruse*

The Velie name became a part of the Deere dynasty in 1860 when John Deere's daughter, Emma, married Stephen H. Velie. In 1863, Velie joined his father-in-law and brother-in-law at the John Deere Plow Works. In 1902, Velie's son, Willard, launched the Velie Carriage Company to manufacture a full line of buggies, carriages, surreys, driving wagons, and spring wagons. *Nick Cedar*

maybe their grandpa's first tractor was a Model A. A few of the John Deere collectors even chose to escape the executive rat race for the chance to farm a few acres as a hobby. In all, John Deere collectors are a diverse group with a similar passion for "bleeding green."

No matter what their reason for collecting John Deere, most of these individuals can be grouped into three general categories based on their experience, expertise, and collecting characteristics. Some collectors may find themselves in a hybrid category somewhere in between the beginner and the extremist. Refer to the collector profile sidebar for a "snapshot" of the various types of John Deere collectors.

The good news is that John Deere collectors as a whole are not competitive to the point of being cutthroat. In general, John Deere collectors enjoy the conquest almost as much as the acquisition. They appreciate the history behind the pieces they buy and value the lasting friendships they've developed. Collectors will often look out for each other, advising against items of questionable authenticity or prices higher than deemed appropriate. In many cases, they even purchase pieces for each other, swapping what one wants for what the other already owns.

Deere Diversity

Thankfully, the smorgasbord of John Deere memorabilia provides collectors with plenty of available options. While this book does not claim to highlight every possible item, it does offer an overview of the variety of John Deere collectibles on the market today. For the sake of organization, these items are grouped into various categories such as promotional items, ephemera, antique iron, and toys. A "catchall" chapter intends to capture the pieces that don't seem to fit neatly into other categories. Some topics, such as toys, belt buckles, watch fobs, wrenches, and marbles, have already been the subject of entire books or specialty magazines. The vast majority of the items in this book, however, have never been in the spotlight before. All in all, more than 1,000 John Deere-related items are featured in the following pages.

Thanks to mice, moisture, and the Mrs., many collectible treasures became kindling for the fire after an ambitious spring cleaning session. Perhaps this elusiveness is what drives the quest to acquire John Deere memorabilia. This book focuses on Deere's agricultural business because it's the primary part of its 160-plus-year history. Also included are miscellaneous mentions of the industrial/construction markets, consumer goods like lawn and garden tractors, and Deere's NASCAR racing sponsorship.

This book's time frame ranges from John Deere's first plow in 1837 all the way up to recently released equipment. Overall, the emphasis is mostly on memorabilia made prior to 1960. Recognizing the wide variety of non-licensed items, this book covers both the unapproved along with the officially licensed items. The book also includes fakes in order to educate collectors on how to distinguish a genuine article from a reproduction. The book also mentions many of the related companies connected to John Deere. In some cases, Deere dealers started marketing these products, then

The Collector Profile

Meet Beginner Bob. As a parts manager at a John Deere dealership, Bob acquired a few "freebies" from souvenirs, awards, and Christmas presents over the past couple of years. Bob soon had more belt buckles than he owned belts. His wife started buying him scale-model toys, and now he has his eye on adding literature to his hobby.

Analysis—Beginning collectors like Bob may not even be aware of their budding habit. They probably own a handful of items assembled mostly by accident, such as through inheritance or receiving something as a gift. They never officially decided to become a John Deere collector . . . it just slowly happened. A "greenhorn" like Bob will come home from an auction wide-eyed and enthusiastic after seeing something new, learning a little about other items, and befriending an experienced collector. Once the collecting bug bites, even beginners can quickly graduate to the status of full-fledged fanatics.

Meet Advanced Adam. He retired five years ago from the Harvester Works factory in Moline. As a Deere & Company employee for more than 20 years, he's gathered quite the collection of memorabilia. He kept many of the things he was given on the job and has always been fascinated by the history of the company. Now that he has "free" time, he's been reading literature and attending auctions within a three-state radius of his home. His collection includes cast-iron seats, wrenches, literature, and service pins.

Analysis—Advanced collectors like Adam have been at it for about five years. They've seen a variety of items and have determined a general direction for their own collection. They don't buy everything they see, but prefer to do the research and make educated decisions before adding an item to their collection. This doesn't prevent them from being duped once in a while, but they tend to chalk it up to learning the game and don't become bitter as a result of a purchasing mistake.

Meet Eddie the Expert. At least that's what fellow collectors call him, although he's too modest to accept the nickname. As a full-time farmer, Eddie found himself restless during the long midwestern winters. His wife encouraged him to find a hobby, so he started collecting John Deere items in the early 1980s when belt buckles were all the rage. He grew disenchanted with it after a few years, and started shopping around for other tiny trinkets and treasures. Before long, he managed to snatch up enough watch fobs, buttons, stickpins, keychains, and pens to fill several display cases. Soon his wife banished his stockpile of stuff to the basement where he could set up a shrine to the Great Green. His kids (and now his grandkids) add to his collection with birthday and Christmas presents, and even buy him "green" gifts for Father's Day. To get his daily dose of Deere, Eddie jumped onto the World Wide Web and found a whole new market for John Deere collectibles online. These days, his spare moments are spent checking e-mail, submitting bids to online auctions, and monitoring sale prices of other memorabilia sold on the Internet.

Analysis—Experts like Eddie have been collecting for more than a decade. In fact, they started before anyone else seemed to be bothering with it. As a result, they were on the receiving end of many strange stares as they paid $5 for a dusty box of assorted junk at a garage sale or flea market. Experts have assembled an extensive collection that usually dominates a spare bedroom, basement, attic, garage, or machine shed. Their spouses either tolerate their habit or join them in their hobby.

Experts revel in the thrill of locating an item they've never seen before and find a way to obtain obscure items others never knew existed. An expert gets several phone calls a night from collector friends asking for help in identifying or authenticating various finds. In fact, expert collectors can spend hours telling stories about the items in their collections, the people they bought them from, and the prices they paid for each item. They'll explain why it was a steal or a bargain, a fair deal, or an overpriced mistake they bought while in the heat of the moment but later regretted.

Meet Harry the Hard-Core Hobbyist. He collects John Deere (and anything popular) and his wife collects Beanie Babies®. Both of them are intense about their hobbies. Harry used to collect classic cars, but then began to hear his friends talk about the growing popularity of John Deere items. He wondered if he shouldn't get in on the action. So he brought his checkbook to a big auction and decided to buy all the "big-ticket" items. He wanted the other collectors to see that he was serious about his new hobby and thought that spending the most money would earn him a place in their circle. He didn't do any research into what an item might be worth—he just bought it, thinking he would worry about values later. As a result of his haphazard ways, Harry has an unorganized, helter-skelter type of a collection. The saddest part is that he doesn't even seem to be having that much fun.

Analysis—Harry falls into the category of an extreme collector. Some say there's a fine line between expert and extreme, but a few would argue otherwise. An extreme collector has made up his or her mind to acquire items deemed of value with no regard for the financial consequences. At an auction, these individuals exhibit bidding fever by running up an item to nearly excessive levels. As a result, their hobby is an expensive one. And what separates the "men from the boys," as they say, is the depth of their pockets when it comes to buying the best memorabilia on the market. While this may put the extreme collector in a different league, other collectors are not always envious of the hard-core hobbyist's deep pockets.

Note: These collector profiles are based purely on speculation and lack scientific support. Any similarities to actual individuals are purely coincidental.

Deere acquired the company. In other examples, the connections are simply related to influential people within the Deere organization.

Naturally, this book is intended for an audience of John Deere collectors. It's very likely that antique dealers and auctioneers will find this book a useful reference as well. But the diversity of John Deere memorabilia can be enjoyed by more than just diehard Deere enthusiasts. Other hobby collectors can find gems too, such as marbles, spoons, postcards, and so on. And collectors of "other color" memorabilia may learn more about their items due to the general similarities in memorabilia from fellow ag equipment manufacturers.

Technology Takes Its Toll

Another interesting facet of this hobby is the way Internet technology impacts the collecting craze. The Internet gives the collector a larger scope beyond his or her local or regional geography to include both national and international markets. In the past, collectors had to put miles on the pickup to attend auctions in person. Diehard Deere collectors would stand in a downpour for hours waiting to give a slight nod to the auctioneer perched on a hayrack. Today's tech-savvy collectors equipped with a computer and modem can surf the Web to shop for John Deere collectibles. By searching for all available online auctions, collectors can connect with buyers and sellers across the globe, not just across the state line. The popularity of these virtual venues will continue to change the collectibles market in the years to come.

A quick search of the World Wide Web finds almost as many hits for John Deere as Beanie Babies®! On any given day, collectors can shop for more than 4,000 John Deere items offered for sale on the Internet. With e-mail and a digital camera, collectors can correspond quickly and visually as opposed to talking on the telephone or mailing photocopies of pieces back and forth. Despite all the positives, there are negative implications in the technologically advanced hobby as well. For example, prices can be inflated and fakes are harder to spot, as scam artists actively pursue the pockets of collectors.

Helpful Hints

For their own protection, collectors should take two key steps prior to purchasing an item. First, authenticate it, if at all possible. If research cannot substantiate the seller's claims, go with gut instinct and hope for the best. Secondly, determine the age of the piece. This can be accomplished by dating the product featured, the logo on it, or the period in which the piece was popular. The "Dating by the Deere" guide helps collectors calculate an appropriate age for any trademarked items.

Valuing John Deere Collectibles

"How much is it worth?" That's the most-asked question concerning John Deere collectibles. Unfortunately, it's not an easy answer, as values are based on a number of factors. An item's rarity is a collective estimate of its availability in the marketplace. An item earns the label "scarce" when several seasoned collectors and experienced auctioneers agree that they have seen very few on the market. This may not be an exact science, but it's the best judge of availability when the manufactured quantity is not a known number.

Another factor in determining an item's value is its condition. General practice with some collectibles is to establish a formal code for denoting the "wear and tear" of a particular piece. In toys, this ranges from "Good" to "New in the Box." Other collectibles use a numerical scale to accomplish the same thing. However, condition ratings can be subjective and may differ between buyer and seller.

Obviously, an item's age also affects its value. A general rule of thumb is, the older the piece, the higher the price. For some reason, items that outlast others merit a premium when it comes to price. Even when manufactured in limited quantities, recently released collectibles are usually less valuable due to their lack of age.

Another way to calculate a collectible's value is by its original pricing. Granted, many items now collected were dealer giveaways and had no associated price per se. Other pieces of memorabilia actually sold for a particular price when first released. If known, the original price may factor into the item's value as a collectible. In some cases, this can at least provide collectors with a reasonable range or ballpark figure.

Naturally, collectible values are driven by demand. Items considered "hot" or desirable by other collectors command higher prices than do pieces of mystery memorabilia. The other intangible is how badly a collector wants to own a piece. On the other side of the coin, it also matters how badly the seller wants to part with it. This delicate dance is hard to gauge and varies greatly depending on the situation and individuals involved.

Dating by the Deer

Since 1876, the leaping deer symbol has served as the identifying icon of Deere & Company. Over its 125-year history, the trademark transformation ranged from the first four-legged leaping-over-the-log deer to the newest two-legged streamlined version. As John Deere's business experienced rapid growth, many of its factories and branch houses created separate identities. A single official trademark was not enforced until the 1960s, although the number of variations seems to be limited after the centennial in 1937. This logo legend will help collectors identify and date trademarked objects.

1876—John Deere's business is almost 40 years old. The deer makes its debut as a four-legged version leaping over a log.

1912—The next "official" progression of the leaping deer shows just three legs, a larger log, and detailed shading in the deer's body. The main wording remains the same, with the addition of "The Trade Mark of Quality Made Famous By Good Implements" below.

1936—Deere's centennial a year later resulted in a number of collectibles bearing this "shield-shaped" logo. The deer again has four legs, but has been simplified to an all-black design. Upon closer inspection, note the longer tail and visible left ear in this artwork.

1937—This slight variation of the trademark is not found all that often. It's the same as the 1936 version but without the shield shape and the "Trade Mark" wording at the very bottom. Some examples use the shaded pattern as shown.

1950—This represents a significant change in the design. The deer still has four legs, but the rear legs are kicked up higher and the rack now points forward instead of backward. The lettering changed as well, with "John Deere" at the top and "Quality Farm Equipment" in a shaded area at the bottom. Collectors often refer to this as the "QFE" logo. Many collectibles sport this trademark design.

1956—The famed four-legged deer logo is simplified further to a black shape with white deer and the words "John Deere". This trademark can be found on many pieces of memorabilia from the late 1950s and 1960s. This trademark is often associated with the "New Generation" tractors introduced in 1960. Although it was used since 1956, the trademark was not officially registered until 1962.

1968—Deere & Company unified its trademark as a sleek two-legged deer. The general black shape became more of a square, but this logo is very similar to the 1956 version. The deer artwork was simplified again with just two legs and a four-point rack pointing forward. With 32 years of reign, this trademark enjoyed the second longest stint in Deere's logo history.

2000—The new millennium marks another new trademark for Deere & Company. The deer is now leaping upward rather than landing and sports sharper edges as well as aggressive styling. The words "John Deere" project a stylish typeface and are now separated from the deer symbol. The outer shape is even more square with shaper outer edges.

Despite the difficulty determining a realistic price range for John Deere collectibles, a Value Guide in Appendix A attempts to answer the inevitable question, "What is it worth?" Because no one person knows the value of everything shown in this book, the price ranges listed are estimated based on the educated guesses of experienced collectors and auctioneers. Research into recent prices realized on the Internet and from other sales has helped create a reasonable range that can be used as a general guide. A final word of advice: Before investing in a piece of John Deere memorabilia, carefully consider all the factors, then consult your gut (and your conscience) to make the final decision.

Trinkets turn into treasures for today's John Deere collectors. Whether it's a pocket watch, tape measure, keychain or ashtray, it's considered collectible on the market for Deere-related memorabilia. Items shown include General-Purpose tractor literature, *Johnny Tractor and His Pals* children's book, Administrative Center flashlight, 1/16-scale Ertl toy Model 60 tractor with 1/16-scale Eska-Carter Model 227 corn picker, Deere CEO William Hewitt's bottle of personal blend scotch whisky, gold flip-top calendar from Venezuela, glass ashtray with Wisconsin dealer imprint, Deere Bicycles trademark replica, Van Brunt Drills 75th anniversary wrench (1986), ruby-red glass paperweight from 1907 Deere company picnic, engraved pocket watch for employee with 50 years of service, jewel-gear pocket watch, Kemp & Burpee Manufacturing stickpin holder, deer leaping over plow watch fob, 1950 trademark logo print block, multiple-ring keychain with dealer imprint, Mixed Car Warehouse Chauffeur badge, and an aluminum pocket tape measure for John Deere Plows. *Nick Cedar*

CHAPTER 2

Promotional Items: Trinkets and Treasures from a Promotional Powerhouse

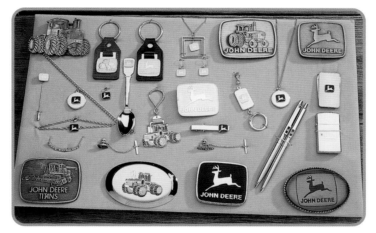

Representing a storied history spanning more than 160 years, the notable "John Deere Green" color quickly identifies Deere & Company agricultural equipment throughout the world. Since 1876, the leaping deer symbol has appeared in all registered trademarks, making it an illustrious icon of the company. Therefore, anything adorned with the leaping deer or colored John Deere green and yellow instantly earns a valuable place in the collectible category of the memorabilia market.

The magnitude of John Deere memorabilia is perhaps best witnessed by the plethora of promotional items produced over the past century and a half. From the beginning, Deere & Company has been a prolific marketer, putting its name on millions of trinkets and treasures. These collectible pieces run the gamut from watch fobs and keychains to matchbooks, belt buckles, pencils, and thermometers. Most items bear the leaping deer symbol in some fashion, along with a Deere-related company name or even a local dealership identity.

It appears that Deere first offered these souvenirs to customers through a coupon system. A 1916 sales flier to dealers explained this method of distribution: "To make sure that farmers appreciate the value of John Deere souvenirs, a small charge is made for them. The usual method of distributing is by placing coupons with the directions for setting up and operating John Deere implements. These coupons when returned with a small amount in stamps or silver, entitle the sender to the souvenir described." Although these items did not cost the dealer anything, the flier did not exactly encourage these promotional efforts. It said, "Souvenirs call attention to something the farmer already knows. They remind him of John Deere goods and the dealer who sells them. They tell no detailed business story and offer no reason for buying the goods they advertise; therefore, their usefulness is somewhat limited."

The Lee Wayne Company of Rockford, Illinois, produced many of the licensed promotional items for John Deere. From belt buckles and key chains to lighters and jewelry, this dealer display case shows a complete set available in the early 1980s. *Nick Cedar*

John Deere Factories of 1950

The John Deere Plow Works in Moline served as headquarters for the entire Deere organization since its construction in 1847. With his original self-polishing design, John Deere's steel plow business grew from 700 plows the first year to 75,000 plows in 1876. Just after the Civil War, this factory was reorganized and incorporated in 1868 as Deere & Company.

The John Deere Harvester Works of East Moline began building grain binders in 1911. First-year production was just 500 units but grew to 320 binders a week in 1915. Additions to the line included corn binders in 1913 and mowers and sulky rakes in 1914. Combines were built in the 1930s, when the plant manufactured the famous Holt combine. In 1939, the No. 12A Combine was introduced followed by self-propelled models after World War II. Today, the Harvester Works still builds John Deere combines — it released the revolutionary 50 Series line in 1999.

The John Deere Planter Works was originally known as the Deere & Mansur Company. Charles Deere, son of John Deere, served as the first president of this company, yet the factory did not become part of Deere's organization until 1911. As early as 1877, the factory built corn planters, and by 1885, they had added stalk cutters, drills, seeders, and a Deere hay rake to the line. From the original edge-drop design to the No. 9 check-row planter introduced in 1901 and the popular No. 999 planter introduced in 1913, later developments would bring speed and accuracy to corn and cotton planting.

The John Deere Van Brunt Works started in 1860 with two brothers (George and Daniel Van Brunt) and their design for a combination seeder and cultivator. Just one year later, the plant moved from Mayville to Horicon, Wisconsin. By 1866, production reached 1,300 seeders and the Van Brunt name earned a worldwide reputation for excellence. In 1911, Deere & Company added the Van Brunt company to its organization.

The John Deere Waterloo Tractor Works was an outgrowth of the Waterloo Gasoline Engine Company, established in 1893 and bought by Deere in 1918. Parent of the famed Waterloo Boy tractor line, this factory manufactured many models of two-cylinder tractors over the years.

The John Deere Des Moines Works came into operation during World War II. Deere & Company purchased the large plant in 1947.

The John Deere Dubuque Tractor Works was built specifically for small farm tractors, which rolled off the line starting in 1947.

The John Deere Wagon Works has its roots in the Moline Wagon Company, which started in 1850 when craftsman James First built wooden wagons by hand. By 1872, the business was incorporated and grew to a capacity of more than 30,000 wagons a year. Around 1880, John Deere sales branches began to sell these wagons and in 1911, John Deere purchased the company and operated it as the Wagon Works factory. According to a 1929 general catalog, "The one thought and aim is to make the John Deere Wagon and other equipment so good that their first cost will eventually be paid in the extra service given."

The John Deere Spreader Works existed from the contributions of two pioneering engineers. August Adams invented the automatic corn sheller in 1859 and established a factory for corn shellers and grain elevators at Marseilles, Illinois. In 1908, Deere contracted with the Marseilles Manufacturing Company to supply corn shellers for the Deere product line. In 1910, Deere & Company took control of Marseilles, moved the plant to East Moline, and changed the name to the Marseilles Company. Joseph Kemp built the first practical manure spreader in 1877 from his base in Syracuse, New York. The Kemp & Burpee Manufacturing Company organized in 1881 and began building spreaders until John Deere purchased the business in late 1910. Shortly after, the "Success" line of manure spreaders gave way to the famed "beater-on-the-axle" manure spreader design that revolutionized the farm implement industry.

The Syracuse Chilled Plow Works of New York state manufactured plows that perfectly complemented John Deere's design for the Midwest. The chilled plows first made by Thomas Wiard in 1867 worked well in the light, gravelly soils of the East. The thriving business became the Syracuse Chilled Plow Company in 1879. First year sales of the highest-grade chilled plows reached 7,000 units. The Hoover line of potato equipment was also built here. In 1911, the Syracuse Chilled Plow Company was added to the John Deere family.

The John Deere Ottumwa Works was the result of a Missouri furniture dealer named Joseph Dain. Worried about hay harvesting problems, he designed, patented, and built hay implements in 1882. A factory at Carrolton, Missouri, moved to Ottumwa, Iowa, in 1900 and became part of Deere & Company in 1911.

The John Deere Welland Works factory in Ontario, Canada, was a subsidiary of the Dain Manufacturing Company, which became part of Deere & Company in 1911.

The Vermilion Malleable Iron Works started at Hoopeston, Illinois, in 1907. Deere & Company purchased the foundry in 1946 to make malleable castings for implements built at factories other than John Deere.

The Union Malleable Iron Works furnished castings to Deere & Company in 1872. It operated as a separate organization until 1911 when Deere purchased it.

The John Deere Killefer Works also resulted from an enterprising individual. John Killefer, a midwestern farmer who relocated to the sandy soils of southern California, found popularity with his heavy-duty, deep-working chisel in 1892. West Coast farmers reveled in this subsoiler's success at shattering compacted soil, which let the rain soak in so yields improved. The Los Angeles factory of Killefer Manufacturing Company became part of John Deere in 1937.

The John Deere Yakima Works in Washington state got its start in 1923 when young Jesse Lindeman designed a special disk harrow for the rolling contours of farmland in the Northwest. He went on to build several orchard tools, spray units, ditchers, subsoilers, and other power farm implements. In 1930, Jesse began to develop a track-type tractor. John Deere furnished the engine and transmission for this popular crawler model. The Lindeman Power Equipment Company joined the John Deere organization in 1947.

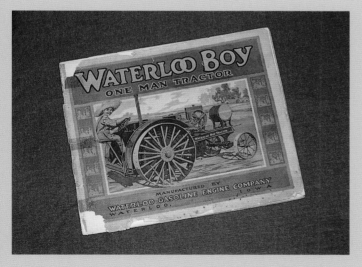

This piece of product literature features the Waterloo Boy "One Man Tractor" that was manufactured at the Waterloo Gasoline Engine Company. John Deere bought the Waterloo, Iowa company in 1918. The artwork on the cover resembles a Model N, which was built between 1917 and 1924. *Brenda Kruse*

These "good-will gifts" eventually gained favor with Deere & Company, as well as its dealers. By 1930, the catalog read: "The use of John Deere souvenirs as gifts to customers has become an established part of the sales-building programs of many John Deere dealers. These dealers have found that judicious distribution of useful articles, bearing John Deere reminders, pays well in added good will that influences sales. Illustrated in this leaflet are practical, attractive items available to John Deere dealers for distribution at fairs, openings, tractor schools and other gatherings, or for keeping on hand at the store for day-to-day customers."

Another paragraph described the positive effect of promotional trinkets: "Presenting a customer with one of the John Deere souvenirs is one effective method of expressing your appreciation. It is the human thing for the customer to feel an increased friendliness in return. He thus tends to become more of an asset on which you can depend. . . . Worth giving and worth having, these souvenirs, as gifts to customers, pay profits in customer loyalty."

Practicality and quality are touted in all advertising specialty catalogs. "The thought that whatever is done to advertise John Deere implements must reflect quality above all things, is not overlooked in the selection of John Deere souvenirs," declared a specialty catalog from 1916.

While some call it crazy, the values placed on these trinkets of yesteryear can be astounding. Surely a dealer would be surprised to discover that his cheap, disposable promotional item is now worth more than the equipment the trinket was intended to promote!

In most cases, dating John Deere items is not as complicated as one might think. The type of logo or trademark used can usually date most John Deere collectibles. Consult the "Dating by the Deer" sidebar in the introduction for details. Other ways to determine the age of an antique include dealership phone numbers, featured product, material used, and the item's era of popularity. The best way to learn how to date memorabilia is to become a historian of Deere & Company's past. A dedicated researcher who pores through the books, articles, catalogs, and other literature can often determine an "official" date that can be supported by documentation. Sometimes a little common sense goes a long way. For example, a 1912 logo on something promoting the centennial in 1936–1937 should raise questions about its authenticity.

Despite the dating dilemmas facing John Deere collectors, most are more concerned about surrounding themselves with the great green-and-yellow rather than solving some of the mysteries associated with their items. For some retired farmers turned collectors, keeping themselves connected to an ag icon like John Deere satisfies the urge to farm the fields. Whatever the reason for collecting John Deere memorabilia, those who "bleed green" will find plenty of promotional items to add to their collections.

Watch fobs held pocket watches long before wristwatches became the standard for time-telling. Fobs, an item all but lost to modern culture, originally enabled a person to keep track of pocket watches and keys. Peak popularity for these ornate medallions attached to leather straps was from about 1900 to 1940. Local dealers generally gave away complimentary key fobs with the purchase of new John Deere equipment.

John Deere offered a fine series of "Genuine Mississippi River Baroque Pearl" fobs from around 1915 to 1940. Both the badge and the buckle are made of a delicate pearl material, which explains why many fobs found today are chipped on the edges or missing the buckle. Another common problem is that the leather strap has been creased and folded enough to tear off. Replacing a strap is a simple repair, so realize that some straps will look much newer as a result.

Given the values placed on these early fobs, many reproductions flood the market. Beware of pieces that do not show consistent wear patterns according to their age. Also look for signs of poor craftsmanship—a good indicator that the item was not an official Deere promotional piece.

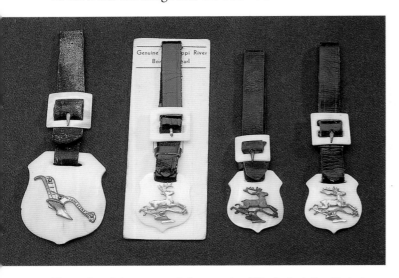

These four fobs represent the popular "Mississippi Pearl" designs. Looking carefully, it's easy to see the slight differences in the leaping-deer logo. Subtleties such as the antlers facing forward or backward, a bent front leg, kicked-up rear legs, and other such details help a trained collector's eye to quickly spot variations in designs. For example, the one attached to its card has the antlers pointed forward, while the two on the right show the rack to the rear. The two fobs on the right may appear identical in deer design, yet they vary in material—one is brass and one is silver. The far left fob uses a larger shield shape with the famed plow emblem, which is inscribed with the words "John Deere." Some collectors have heard that these special fobs were worn by "Block Men," which are yesterday's version of Territory Managers. *Nick Cedar*

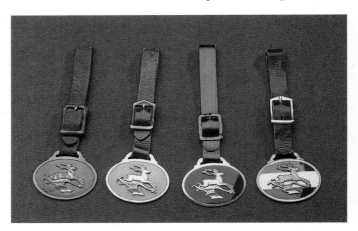

Above: These four fobs constitute a series that collectors crave because of the challenge of finding all four in good condition. The colored enamel background comes in black, royal blue, powder blue, and a unique red-white-and-blue-striped version. A second variation of this flaglike fob also exists with differences in the deer. Made between 1910 and 1940, these colored fobs might have represented the various factories of Deere & Company at the time. Others suspect the different colors referred to the years of release or the branch that gave them away. According to seasoned collectors, each of these fobs is reasonably rare, but the black one is the hardest to find. Yet this one is heavily advertised as a "goodwill gift" in catalogs dating 1916, 1930, 1935, and 1940. These make no mention of other colored versions. In a 1930 dealer ad specialties catalog, a caption reads, "The silver nickel-plated figure on this fob contrasts attractively with onyx-enamel background." It was even called "indestructible" in a 1916 souvenir flier. Judging by their existence yet today, this claim can certainly be upheld. *Nick Cedar*

Left: These fobs show an assortment of designs over the years. The first one uses a unique type of strap and leatherwork. There is some controversy surrounding this medallion featuring the giant letter "D" with the deer poking its head through it. Some collectors believe it is an early fob from the buggy days with the 1880 trademark; others think it may be a recently issued reproduction. The second fob represents the 1936 trademark with its special shield shape and black grooved background. Another version of this design does not have the lines in the background. Other collectors have located a variation showing a larger deer and oversized lettering. This relatively rare fob is advertised in dealer specialty catalogs from 1930 to 1940. The caption in a 1930 flier reads: "The fob illustrated above is of dull black jet finish, with the John Deere trade-mark faced off bright—something new in watch fob finishes. Price, 10 cents each, plus postage." The third fob is an early pewter design with the hat-wearing Waterloo Boy and tractor. The far right fob is an ornate gold-plated design with colorful Model D on a celluloid background. Collectors presume these last two designs to be quite rare, dated between 1915 and 1920. *Nick Cedar*

Another sampling of fobs displays variety in age and design. The first one on the left appears to be quite similar to the official trademark used today, but upon closer inspection, you can see that the deer has four legs, with the rack pointed straight up as on the 1956 logo. Yet this is actually a more recent design produced by Deere in the 1980s. A variation with a flat deer also exists. The middle one is a round pendant with the deer leaping over the plow. Notice how its front leg is bent up and the rack points backwards. The wording at the bottom simply says, "Moline, Ill." On the reverse is the bust of Deere with the words, "He gave the world the steel plow." Note its coinlike edges and older-style strap linkage. Collectors presume this fob to be an early one, and thus quite rare. The far right fob is shown with the back side of the badge, which states, "First Class Goods. John Deere Plows, Cultivators, Velie Buggies Etc." The front is less identifiable as John Deere—it features the Butts Building, an early branch office in Wichita, Kansas. *Nick Cedar*

Some special fobs featured bright colors for added appeal. The red shield on the left has a four-legged deer in gold on a white square-fob shape. Ornate gold detailing at the bottom adds to its beauty. A white and green version of this 1980s design also exists. The fob on the right uses an older logo design with the year 1876 at the bottom. The reverse states it was given out at the 31st International Show, April 21–23, 1995, in Strongsville, Ohio. *Nick Cedar*

Keychains eventually replaced key fobs as promotional gifts. Today, keychains are still widely available as promotional items from dealers. This collection shows the variety of designs issued over the years. Upper left: A brass teardrop keychain highlights the 530 and 430 round balers introduced in 1983. Lower left: This square design identifies a four-wheel-drive tractor and the Tractor Works plant. Upper middle: The large yellow multiple-ring keychain is old enough to feature the four-legged deer logo used from 1956 to 1967. Lower middle: The smaller square also displays the four-legged deer, but on a yellow background. Upper right: This keychain promotes tractor manufacturing at Deere with the phrase "The Tradition Lives On." Lower right: This uniquely shaped keychain uses a newer design with the latest trademarked logo. *Nick Cedar*

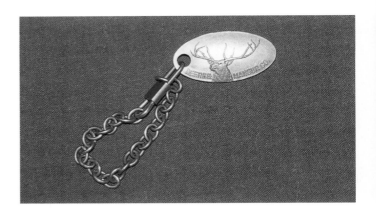

These fobs promote the Moline Wagon Company, which became part of Deere & Company in 1910. The wagon wheel and greyhound were the trademark symbols of this "light running and durable" equipment. *Nick Cedar*

This unusual piece appears to be a key fob of sorts, although its exact purpose is unknown. In 1877, Alvah Mansur and Charles Deere joined forces to manufacture corn planters under the name of the Deere & Mansur Company. This was close enough to the co-partnership name in Kansas City (Deere, Mansur & Company) to cause confusion at the time, and it still does today. Until 1909, Deere & Mansur was a wholly separate company, but sold its planters under the Deere label through Deere branch houses. The deer with the large rack closely resembles the trademark design used by the Minneapolis branch in the late 1890s. The wording on the back of this oval tag says, "corn planters, disc harrows, hay loaders, etc." *Brenda Kruse*

Many people do not associate the name Velie with John Deere, yet the Velie family was very involved in the Deere business and also manufactured a variety of vehicles on its own. The Velie name was associated with carriages by 1902, motor trucks starting in 1911, automobiles from 1908 to 1928, tractors between 1916 and 1920, and even airplanes in 1928. These four fobs show the two major versions of Velie fob designs. The round "wheel-type" with "The Name Insures Quality" slogan and the large "letter V" version can be dated prior to 1928. *Nick Cedar*

An even easier promotional item for mass manufacture and marketing is the pin, ranging from simple stickpins to lapel pins, hat pins, tie tacks, and pin-backed buttons. While thousands of these were often made at once, some of the rarest finds involve early or outdated products such as Deere bicycles, or related companies and brands, such as Dain, Moline Wagon, and Velie.

With the number of years, products, people, dealerships, and events involved, the number of possible combinations makes pins and buttons an easy place to start with a collection. These types of treasures are usually discovered at the bottom of drawers or in boxes of miscellaneous junk at garage sales. Some of the stickpins break easily, but buttons are durable items that can last many decades in good condition. At first glance, these pins and buttons may seem similar or simple, but reading the fine print or studying the designs may lead to a rare find well worth the investigation.

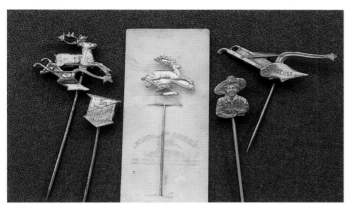

Lapel stickpins come in all sizes and shapes. Here are five examples of the variety in designs. The first one has the familiar deer leaping over the plow. The second one from the left is a small shield with a four-legged deer and the words "John Deere Plow Co., St. Louis, Mo." This design is identical to what experts believe is the first known John Deere watch fob. The middle stickpin on its original card shows the differences between leaping deer designs. Note how the areas between the legs, belly, and antlers are solid, not cut out like the one on the far left. There are also several versions in varying sizes. Promoted as "not too costly for wide distribution," these stickpins were advertised in specialty catalogs of 1916, 1930, 1935, and 1940, from which dealers could order 100 stickpins for $2.50 in 1930, or for $5 in 1940. The smaller pin on the right is the hat-wearing Waterloo Boy with those words inscribed in his hat brim. This design is also presumed to be quite rare. The far right stick pin is the steel plow, but with the word "Syracuse" on the share. This represents the Syracuse Chilled Plow Company, which John Deere purchased in 1911. Experienced collectors claim this version is quite scarce. *Nick Cedar*

This special sampling of pins denotes how related companies fit into the John Deere product line. The larger red-and-gold "Great Dain" pin refers to Dain hay equipment, officially acquired by Deere in late 1910. The two stickpins (front center) feature the Moline Wagon Company, also a part of Deere & Company starting in 1910. Both pins are very similar with their spoked wheel design and greyhound in the middle, but slight differences in design and wording can be seen upon closer inspection. The upper right stickpin is considered very old, as it promotes the first corn planters from John Deere. The Deere & Mansur Company manufactured a rotary design in 1877. The pin features an ear of corn with a deer inside the end of a corncob. The phrase "Corn Planters" is spelled out in the kernels. This design closely matches a trademark used in 1907. *Nick Cedar*

This dangling celluloid pin promotes the idea that "John Deere Plows Make Better Seedbeds." The other stickpin is also associated with Deere, although it represents the Grand Detour Plow Company of Dixon, Illinois. John Deere's original blacksmith shop in Grand Detour, Illinois, first gave birth to his famed plow design in 1837. Deere's partnership with Leonard Andrus was dissolved in 1847 when Deere moved to Moline. Andrus continued manufacturing plows under the name of the Grand Detour Plow Company, which later moved to Dixon. A predecessor to the J.I. Case Company acquired it in 1919. *Brenda Kruse*

These three items represent a variety of uses, promotional efforts, and products. The chrome-plated leaping deer tie clasp on its original card is listed in a 1935 souvenir catalog. It said, "Any man would like to get one of these attractive, latest style clasps." The plow pin on the card was shown in specialty catalogs as early as 1916. The 1930 flier said, "The gold-plated John Deere plow pin, pictured above, is a favorite for special distribution to the womenfolk. Price 15 cents each, plus postage." By 1940, the price was up to 25 cents each. The red-white-and-blue flag advertises "John Deere Plows. The World Standard." with a unique front-facing deer logo in the white circle on a blue background with four stars. Knowledgeable collectors estimate this prized piece to be from the late 1800s or early 1900s. *Nick Cedar*

John Deere dealers often handed out promotional objects like these at fairs, shows, and other special events. Note the range in size and design, as well as age and value. The large orange button (ca. 1920s) promotes "Cory Hardware Co., Furniture and Undertaking, John Deere Implements, Repairs for All Machinery, Elkhart, Iowa, Ernest G. Cory." On the reverse side, this piece is a whetstone for sharpening cutlery or tools. The smaller white button (ca. 1920s) says "THE FAIR. JOHN DEERE. Meet us at Sedalia Oct. 1 to 7." A colorful design shows the Waterloo Boy and tractor (ca. 1917–1918). The navy blue button with red lettering is quite scarce. "If You Love Me, Grin! Deere Bicycles" is imprinted on the button, but the word "Bicycles" below the deer has been scratched off this extremely rare design (ca. 1890s). The tiny white button also promotes "Deere Bicycles" with the front-facing deer logo (ca. 1890s). Whitehead & Hoag Co. made this white button (ca. 1880s) showing Deere's bust and stating "Inventor of the Steel Plow. John Deere." Also made by Whitehead & Hoag, this unique button shows a large "D" with a deer in the center. The words "Up-To-Date" are at the top, "John Deere Plow Co. Kansas City" is at the bottom, and "Saddles, Harness, Collars," are within the letter "D." Experienced collectors believe this is a rare pin from 1896. The large white button is actually a celluloid pocket mirror that says "The 'New-Way' Air Cooled. Goes and Goes Right." at the top, and "John Deere Plow Co. Kansas City" at the bottom. Several branches sold these engines, resulting in different regional versions of these mirrors. *Nick Cedar*

Belt Buckles Abound

Considered a major collector category in itself, belt buckles reached their prime in the 1980s. Because of the sheer number of designs issued in addition to non-licensed versions, only a few of the earliest or rarest buckles have held their value. However, extensive production makes belt buckles an ideal starting point for any interested collector. In fact, buckles are often how collectors get their start.

Belt buckles range in size, shape, design, and in the product or place honored. Buckles can be gold-, silver-, or nickel-plated, brass, bronze, pewter, even cast-iron, leather, or wood laser craft. Some have an antique finish, while others have colorful cloisonne or epoxy inserts. Shapes vary from rectangles and squares to ovals and circles.

Buckles were issued at dealer shows and meetings, as well as for special awards, such as the FFA Walking Plow or the Super Service Award from the Portland Branch. Unique designs include a 1980 buckle that commemorated the line of John Deere snowmobiles in use at Lake Placid in New York for the Winter Olympics.

Special designs to honor specific products came from the Hay Masters, Des Moines, Moline, and Waterloo factories. Foreign buckles hail from Australia, Mexico, and Canada. Standard buckles were sold at John Deere dealerships. These include designs featuring combines, tractors, John Deere Day, industrial equipment, and the "Nothing Runs Like a Deere" slogan. Other buckles include special Two-Cylinder Club designs, as well as dealer-specific buckles. An extensive series of "unofficial" cloisonne designs even sport a colorful epoxy swirl background.

For additional details about previously released buckles, consult *The Complete Guide to Collecting John Deere Buckles*, by Frances Kavalier and Roger Hintz, published by Toy Farmer Publications in 1992.

These three examples of belt buckles also come with matching key-chains. The upper left pewter design features the four-wheel-drive 8630 tractor introduced in 1975. The gold-plated one (upper right) commemorates "Three Million Diesel Engines" made from 1949 to 1990. The bottom pewter buckle honors the employees of a specific group at the Plow & Planter Works from 1979–1984. The Centennial and Macombers divisions were off-site machining operations located in Rock Island, Illinois. *Nick Cedar*

This quartet represents some of the gold-plated buckles from a newer trademark series that started in 1980. The upper left buckle (made in 1983) displays an 1875-style logo with a four-legged deer leaping over a log. There are also two silver versions of this half-moon-shaped buckle. The round buckle (upper right) shows four models of John Deere tractors in 1982. A silver version also exists in this design. The large buckle (lower right) highlights four pieces of industrial equipment from 1974. The lower left buckle from 1988 features the Deere bicycles logo in an antique-brass finish. *Nick Cedar*

This assortment of buckles shows the leaping deer in various stages of age. The lower black and silver buckle with four-legged deer is believed to be the very first John Deere belt buckle issued with employee uniforms in the late 1940s and early 1950s. Made by Hamlin Manufacturing in Greensboro, North Carolina, this scarce buckle is the most valuable design today. To its right, a newer 1980s-style dress belt buckle features the trademark symbol used from 1968 to 2000. The far left buckle uses the 1936 shield logo and even shows some wear, but is dated 1984 on the back. A larger version of this silver-plated buckle also exists. The top buckle is a simple design made by a Plow-Planter employee in his spare time. The far right buckle is a large silver-and-green design rumored to be the creation of a Wyoming prisoner in the 1990s. Although some of these were not officially licensed merchandise from Deere, these handmade designs are quite unique and can be collected as well. *Nick Cedar*

These four belt buckles further display the variety of sizes, colors, shapes, and details over the years. The lower left one (made in 1990) is a colored brass oval showcasing the Waterloo Boy kerosene tractor of 1914–1924. The upper left one celebrates the centennial of *The Furrow* magazine (1895–1995) and came complete with a black velvet bag. The upper right silver-plated buckle was issued in honor of the 150th anniversary of the Deere & Company (1837–1987). The lower right design is a special issue from the 1987 Thresher's Bee given by the Threshermen Collectors of Albert City, Iowa. *Nick Cedar*

Pens and pencils are typical tokens of appreciation from a local dealership. Often handed out at fairs, sales meetings, and other events, pens and pencils went quickly into customers' pockets and purses, as well as decorated the desks and counters of dealerships. Bullet pencils may be the most creative find of any, as these stubby, capped writing utensils seem to represent days past. Traditional #2 stick pencils were eclipsed by fancier mechanical pencils over the years.

As with any John Deere collectible, the best way to date these writing instruments is by the style of leaping deer on the logo. Others list simple two- or three-digit phone numbers for the local dealership—another indicator of age.

Perhaps even more amazing is that some of these antiques still write!

Many collectors seek out specific dealerships from their local area, region, or state. Others are simply drawn to the pearlized designs or catchy marketing slogans like "A Good Point to Work Safely." Still others find unique combinations of brands like John Deere, Maytag, Studebaker, and Frigidaire sharing space on a single pen or pencil.

Since pens and pencils are considered by most collectors to be an inexpensive, lower-value category, their abundance makes them a prime starting point for a budding collector interested in capturing bits and pieces of company history.

These pearlized mechanical pencils make an impressive addition to any collection. Some designs promoted pieces of equipment like the New Generation tractor from 1960, as shown on the top pencil. Others were decorated with logos, such as the Quality Farm Equipment (QFE) version that made its debut in 1950, and then the simpler four-legged deer version starting in 1956. The industrial division of Deere issued promotional items as well, although these are often more difficult to find than agricultural items. *Nick Cedar*

An assortment of pens and pencils of varying styles and ages displays the diversity of designs. The top pencil from the John Deere Plow Company features a hybrid logo most similar to the 1912 logo, but within the shield shape added to the design by 1936. The bottom bullet pencil honors the centennial celebration in 1937. Several of the imprints use the QFE logo, which was designated as the official trademark from 1950 to 1955. Other famous brand names such as Studebaker, Frigidaire, and Maytag help date these items. The mechanical pencil that promotes Power Steering can be dated to the 1953 introduction of the 70 Series tractors. *Nick Cedar*

This trio of older pens can be easily dated between 1956 and 1967 due to the four-legged leaping deer. The top two green-and-yellow designs are inscribed with "John Deere Malleable Works," a foundry supplier for Deere back to 1872 when it was named Union Malleable. Deere acquired this casting supplier in 1911. Malleable Works closed its doors when the new John Deere Foundry opened in 1968. *Nick Cedar*

Before the flame was associated with smoking cigarettes or cigars, it primarily provided light and heat to early generations. Eventually, John Deere began promoting itself with smoker's supplies, such as matchbooks and matchsafes, butane lighters, and even ashtrays. Early matchbooks were often colorful and creative. Some even had images of tractors printed directly on the matches themselves. Lighters began as crude wick-based capsules and graduated to square-shaped flip-top models. Made by recognizable brand names such as Zippo and Scripto, these "sure-fire friend winners" can even be found in the collections of non-smokers today.

Here is an example of both types of matches—books for paper matches and safes for wooden matches. The colorful two-cylinder tractor design is a rare find, as most books have had the matches removed. Finding a book with all the matches intact is quite a feat. The sterling silver matchsafe box on the right uses the gold leaping deer logo that is identical to stickpin designs, yet the safe cannot be authenticated. *Nick Cedar*

These "Feature" matchbooks are more interesting open than closed. Inside, the Model A is printed directly on the matches. Note the styled two-cylinder tractor with spoked wheels and early rubber tires. The matchbook on the right is personalized with "Iowa State Fair 1938" on its outer cover. *Nick Cedar*

A trio of cigarette lighters from John Deere's early days again shows the famed four-legged deer design. The Zippo lighter on the left shows the Quality Farm Equipment logo. A dealer imprint of "Robert P. Flynn, Morrice, Michigan" completes the design. The far right lighter also features the older four-legged leaping deer with the marketing slogan "Sparks New Earning Power" on it. The shiny gold lighter in the middle honors 125 years of Deere (1962) and includes the tin case from Scripto. *Nick Cedar*

Ashtrays were also promotional items associated with John Deere. The white porcelain ashtray shows the Quality Farm Equipment logo with four-legged deer. The ashtray has a slot to keep a book of matches within easy reach. The matchbook features "Vitrea 45% nitrogen," the result of a brief venture with a fertilizer plant in Oklahoma from 1952 to 1965. The other ashtray also includes a holding place for a box of matches. The dealer imprint is from the "Broward-Palm Beach Tractor Co., Pompano Beach/Boynton Beach" out of Florida. *Nick Cedar*

This assorted collection of lighters spans the years and the country with Oklahoma, Texas, Iowa, and Washington imprints. Top row, left to right: Green with yellow lettering: "Heaton Implement, Edinburg, Texas"; Brushed chrome Zippo with "John Deere Intercontinental Ltd. Washington Office"; High-polish chrome Zippo in original box with four-legged leaping deer logo; Chrome with Quality Farm Equipment logo. Middle row left to right: Wellington lighter in original box with black-and-yellow industrial equipment design for "Earthmoving-Logging" qualifies as rare—selling for $200 at a recent auction; Chrome with four-legged deer logo and "Wade" dealership imprint and phone number (452-6918); Chrome with stoplight icon and "Work Smarter, Not Harder, It's Easier. John Deere." Bottom row, left to right: Gold with tractor design and dealer imprint "Jones Whorton Implement Co., Hollis, Okla."; Red with black cap bullet lighter (ca. 1915) promoting "John Deere Tractor Co. Waterloo, Iowa"; Gold dress design that says "To A Matchless Friend From Gochenour Implement Co., Pocahontas, Iowa"; Green-and-gold lighter with four-legged deer logo. *Nick Cedar*

A trio of ashtrays promotes John Deere and its dealers in the late 1950s. The large white round ashtray has three gold four-legged deer on the bottom. The glass ashtray on the lower left is from "John Deere Sales and Service. Watertown Implement Co. Phone 874. Watertown, Wis. Clarence Gartzke." The glass one on the right is "Compliments of Rudy, Fisher Implement Co." A similar version was advertised in a 1966 specialty catalog. *Nick Cedar*

Over the years, a variety of measuring devices served as promotional tools for John Deere. You'll find the leaping deer logo or dealership insignia imprinted on a number of tape measures, rulers, yardsticks, levels, and even snow gauges. Perhaps the most desired collectible in this category is the pocket tape measure, which is an ideal size for women's purses. Many of these miniature measures came in colorful celluloid cases.

Rulers and yardsticks made an easy promotional gimmick for local dealerships, as every home kept at least one within reach—some for measuring, others for disciplinary reasons. Rarer still are bubble levels for a customer's shop. Rain gauges of today are not at all rare, but early versions measuring snowfall equivalents are certainly unique.

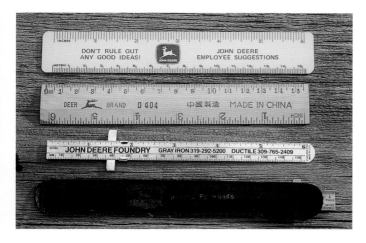

These four pocket-sized rulers come from a variety of places. The top yellow one is from Deere corporate and states "Don't Rule Out Any Good Ideas! John Deere Employee Suggestions." The wooden ruler was "Made in China" and even includes Chinese writing, but mistakenly identifies John Deere as "Deer Brand" with a unique version of the leaping deer. The stainless steel slide rule comes from the John Deere Foundry and lists "Cast Iron 319-292-5200" and "Ductile 309-764-2409." The bottom one is a stainless steel slide rule tucked inside a black velvet pouch imprinted with the Quality Farm Equipment logo and "Harvester Works" in blue ink. *Nick Cedar*

Dating back to 1902 and 1904, these two aluminum cases may be the oldest examples of John Deere tape measures. The slightly smaller one on the left states "John Deere Plow Co., St. Louis–Dallas–New Orleans" on the outer rim. At the top, above the four-legged, log-leaping deer is: "John Deere Plows. Full Line Farm Tools." On either side of the log are the dates 1847 and 1902. "We Solicit Your Mail Orders" is written below. The larger tape measure on the right is imprinted along the outer rim, "The Deere Vehicles. Made at our factory in St. Louis." Above the shield logo states, "World's Fair 1904." Apparently the one on the left is the prototype and the one on the right was released as an official promotional piece. The reverse of the prototype is the same design as the tape measure on the right, minus the wording, "World's Fair 1904." *Nick Cedar*

This collection of tape measures includes a special series of logo-adorned celluloid cases, much valued by collectors today. Two of these tape measures have early patent dates of 11-4-10 and 7-10-17, yet the logos are from 1912 and 1950. The upper right tape measure features the bust of John Deere, which is on the reverse of this series as shown in specialty catalogs from 1930, 1935, and 1940. "This long-wearing, 48 inch tape measure is one of the most useful and most appreciated of the JOHN DEERE gifts. Well-marked JOHN DEERE trademarks, plus bright yellow and green colors make this an attractive gift at a cost of 20 cents each, plus postage," stated the 1940 leaflet. The price in 1930 was just 10 cents each, and the caption read: "Long-wear is insured in the construction of the tape-measure pictured above. The ivory band encasing the tape is held securely between the celluloid top and bottom without the use of glue. There is no falling apart due to glue growing brittle with age." Judging from the condition of these, that claim holds true yet today. Quite similar in design, the lower left tape measure shows the four-legged deer logo on both sides, which dates it sometime after 1956 and before 1968. The larger one in the center is a Deere & Webber Company trademark from Minneapolis, Minnesota. This special item could date back to 1918, making it of considerable potential value. *Nick Cedar*

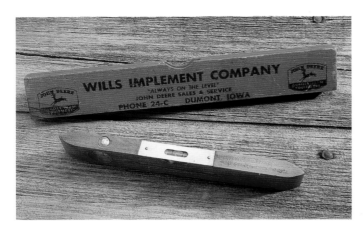

The large red level is from "Wills Implement Company" which is "Always on the Level" with "John Deere Sales & Service" from "Dumont, Iowa." Note the simple phone number (Phone 24-C) and the QFE logo, which puts it around 1950. The wooden level on the bottom is hard to read due to wear, but is engraved "John Deere Malleable Works" with the marketing slogan "Be On the Level With Safety." *Nick Cedar*

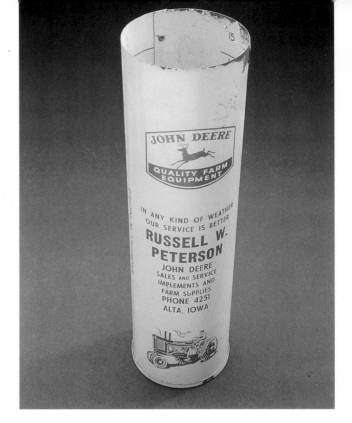

This 15-inch-tall tin tube is an early device for measuring precipitation. The cylindrical gauge shows snowfall in inches with its rainfall equivalent. The Quality Farm Equipment logo and a Model A tractor give this tall yellow tube a date of around 1950. "In any kind of weather our service is better" boasts "Russell W. Peterson, John Deere Sales and Service, Implements and Farm Supplies. Phone 4251. Alta, Iowa." *Nick Cedar*

A cubed yardstick from a "John Deere Dealer" joins a beautiful three-piece wooden walking stick. The brass knob on the end is engraved with a two-legged, leaping-deer logo. According to a collector, these were given out at the Minnesota State Fair in the early 1970s. *Nick Cedar*

Although not everyone is able to identify these two measuring devices, the bolt sizer and plow share gauge certainly came in handy on the farm. The 7-inch cast tool offers both inch and metric scales. At the top, the combined letters "JD" and a part number (P1622) identify it as a John Deere piece. The words "Shares Measure Up" are inscribed in the body of the ruler. The colorful metal measuring device includes a bolt sizer at the top, an 8-inch ruler on the right side, and a step gauge on the third side. Compliments of "Grover Implement" in "Amboy, Minnesota," this promotional item sports a four-legged deer logo and the Model 530 tractor along with images of bolts and a drill bit. Made by the Vernon Company of Newton, Iowa, this piece is probably from 1959 or 1960. *Michelle Schueder*

Cutting-Edge Promotional Items

Pocket knives and letter openers have long been considered effective promotional tools. Issued by John Deere, these convenient tools are now collectible items of value. As most farmers know, a pocketknife is an invaluable tool to have handy at all times. Naturally, a John Deere letter opener makes a helpful addition to any desk. Some of these come straight from the desks of company employees at corporate headquarters in Moline. Some pocket tools perform dual duty as a knife blade and letter opener. Others are Swiss Army style, packed with convenient tools. However, these items are easily reproduced, and fakes are abundantly available, so buyer beware!

The top two letter-openers feature "Mother of Pearl" bodies with logos dating from 1950 to 1967. These combination tools also include a pull-out knife blade. The larger yellow Swiss Army-style pocket tool simply says "John Deere" in green. The small round white one to the right is from "Siemon Implement" of "Belle Plaine, Minn." The other yellow pocketknife (upper far right) is suspect—probably a laser-cut reproduction despite its leaping-over-the-log deer logo. The black-and-silver switchblade at the bottom also appears old because of its early logo, yet a lack of wear (among other hints) suggests this is much newer . . . and therefore, a possible fake. *Nick Cedar*

Signs of the Times

Signs are probably one of the most visible of John Deere collectibles. As a retail environment, dealership walls were filled with them. From the famed leaping-deer logo to the signature green and yellow, signage at the local dealership must meet certain requirements as part of corporate identity standards. Some signs were used as advertising efforts, while others identified departments within the dealership. Other signs were offered to proud owners of John Deere equipment to promote their loyalty to the Great Green. These often graced mailboxes, gates, and fence posts at the end of the lane or were tacked up on the barn or granary.

Naturally, a number of variations exist, namely with different leaping-deer logos. To keep all dealers up-to-date, a "dress-up" program regularly retires some signs, boosting their value as a collectible. However, not all signs were company-issued, either. Sometimes a dealer would order a special custom-made sign. In addition, John Deere's regional sales branches used to operate as somewhat separate entities in the past, so several signs are specific to these areas. A few rarer product-based signs include ones for John Deere lawn and garden tractors and snowmobiles.

Authentic signs can be quite large, and many show signs of weathering, with rust, peeling paint, and scratched enamel. Early paint did not hold up well under hours of scorching sunlight or other demonstrations of Mother Nature's wrath. One way to date these signs is by the material used. Early signs were wooden, cardboard, or tin. Porcelain, enamel, and pressed metal signs came next, followed by lighted signage, and finally neon, revolving, or other fancy creations. Today, advertising signage includes banners, plastic signs, stickers, window clings, and even magnetic signs.

This sign for John Deere Parts measures 5 x 28 inches. The Quality Farm Equipment logo dates this sign to around 1950. It reads "Buy Genuine John Deere Parts. Exact Duplicates in Fit . . . Quality . . . Performance." This sign recently sold at an auction for $350—a price some collectors consider unreasonably high. *Nick Cedar*

Perhaps the most famous John Deere sign is this 2 x 6-foot rectangular one in black with red-and-yellow lettering. Manufactured by the Veribrite Sign Company of Chicago, these signs went through a baking process to put porcelain or enamel over the steel. Unfortunately, the finish is brittle and chips easily, making a sign in mint condition a real challenge to find. Some signs are double-sided, which can add to their value. This version is known as the three-legged deer; a four-legged one also exists. These signs probably hung in John Deere dealerships between the 1910s and 1940s. *Nick Cedar*

Signage for dealer identity, plus advertising, publicity, and promotion has been (and will be) a key area of John Deere collectibles. Any collector would be proud to hang a sign of loyalty on the walls surrounding his or her prized collection. Unfortunately, reproductions run rampant in this area, so beware. If you do want to add a certain sign to your collection, be sure the price you knowingly pay for a fake is nowhere near the amount an original might bring.

This sign apparently identified a particular area of the Deere garage along Third Avenue in Moline. Made of painted steel, the 24-inch square sign uses the four-legged logo, which gives a clue as to its age (ca. 1956-1968). *Denny Eilers*

From pocket watches and wristwatches to wall clocks and alarm clocks, time-keeping devices were ideal promotional giveaways for John Deere. These "timely" reminders of the company and dealership served as practical souvenirs that customers could put to good use. Knowing the outside temperature has always been an important factor in farming, which has made thermometers an ideal good-will gift from John Deere dealers to customers. Even today, thermometers are popular promotional items.

This large green-and-yellow clock features the four-legged deer logo, making it between 1956 and 1968. Measuring 17x14 inches, this clock still keeps time despite its 30-plus years. *Nick Cedar*

These three dress pocket watches could be as old as 1956, as calculated by the four-legged leaping deer on the two outer watches. The middle watch appears to be of similar vintage, but is of a slightly different style, and the leaping deer has only two legs, making it after 1968. Note how these designs do not say "John Deere" anywhere on them—the leaping deer alone identifies the brand. These watches are called "jewel backs," meaning they use a jewel as a pivoting point. *Nick Cedar*

A rare find from any company's history, this gold-filled pocket watch was given to an employee for 50 years of service with Deere & Company. The engraving states: "Presented to Charles L. Edlund in Appreciation 50 Years of Loyal Service. John Deere Plow Works. 1890-1940." Earning this watch was quite an accomplishment, as is owning it today as a priceless collectible. *Nick Cedar*

This antique "Big Ben" alarm clock by Westclox from 1923 features the Model D tractor on its face. Certain details are called out around the tractor, such as "Steering Wheel," "Spade Lug," "Belt Pulley," and "Fuel Tank." Deere built a prototype of the Model D in 1923. Early versions (1924–1925) were known as the "spoker D" because of the spoked flywheel; the solid flywheel design started in 1926. Several versions of these antique alarm clocks have been found, including one featuring the Waterloo Boy. Experts warn collectors that these and similar pieces are being reproduced. *Nick Cedar*

This handy invention was a forerunner to today's wristwatches that include a small date window. These mini-calendars attached to a watch-band to give an entire month at a glance. Compliments of John Deere Finance, these convenient calendars encouraged dealers to promote the John Deere Credit Plan in 1967 and 1968. *Denny Eilers*

Popular promotional tools for local dealers, thermometers imprinted with specific dealership names and locations are prevalent. The smaller one on the left is a unique version because it lists "Caterpillar" in addition to displaying the Quality Farm Equipment logo. "Johnson Tractor Co." of "Ontario – RIVERSIDE – Coachella" gave its California customers an easy way to remember the dealership. The larger one on the right depicts a styled Model A tractor with driver from "Belanger & Howard Sales & Service." To contact this dealership, simply "Phone 100" or visit them in "Geneseo, Ill." *Nick Cedar*

Seemingly identical in design (as well as temperature reading), these twin thermometers vary slightly upon closer inspection. At the bottom, the right one says "Nothing Runs Like A Deere," while the left one says "Deere, C'est Tout Dire. Fabriqué aux Etats-Unis." These French phrases translate into "Deere is the Best. Made in the USA." *Nick Cedar*

Mirror, mirror on the wall, who's the "deerest" of them all? While not a popular item today, visor mirrors were an ideal promotional gift before car manufacturers began making them standard equipment. Other hanging or pocket mirrors were popular with women. Some mirrors included thermometers. In general, mirrors from the 1940s bring around $100 today.

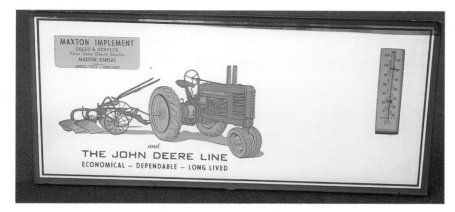

Above: This mirror highlights the Model A tractor with plow and "The John Deere Line. Economical–Dependable–Long Lived." To date this mirror, simply analyze the tractor. A styled design makes it as old as 1938, and the absence of a cushioned seat means it was probably made before 1947. The dealer imprint area says "Maxton Implement Sales & Service, Your John Deere Dealer, Maxton, Kansas, Sample 475122 – John Deere." Because another nearly identical version without a thermometer also exists, this gives the impression that this version was simply a sample and that Deere chose to purchase the one without the thermometer. Either way, a "salesman's sample" item often adds value to a collection given its rarity and possibility of never being officially produced by Deere. *Nick Cedar*

Right: This creative mirror/thermometer urges a customer to "Keep Me" at the top. Inside the two circles within the horseshoe are a four-leaf clover with the words "I bring you good luck" and a 1937 penny with the words "You'll never be broke." At the bottom is a dealer imprint area: "Compliments of Tredway Implements, Your John Deere Dealer, Harlan, Iowa," with a Quality Farm Equipment logo. At first glance, one would be tempted to date this back to 1937 due to the penny, but the QFE logo wasn't introduced until 1950. The penny choice probably related to the centennial Deere celebrated in 1937. *Nick Cedar*

Left: Perhaps the most stunning of any mirrored collectible is the celluloid "Many Brands" desk mirror. Measuring 5 inches in diameter, the face of this unique mirror displays 10 different company logos—all of which eventually became a part of Deere & Company. Experts date this prized piece around 1911, which is when Deere acquired the majority of these companies. Brands under the John Deere Plow umbrella include (left to right): Fort Smith Wagons ("From Forest to Farm"); Velie Motor Vehicles ("The Name Ensures the Quality"); Velie Carriage Company ("Wrought Iron"); Syracuse Plows ("Best in Earth"); Dain Manufacturing Company of Ottumwa, Iowa ("Great Dain Line"); Deere & Mansur Company of Moline, Illinois; Marseilles Company of East Moline, Illinois; Moline Wagon Company of Moline, Illinois; Van Brunt Manufacturing Company of Horicon, Wisconsin; and Davenport Wagon Company of Davenport, Iowa ("Roller Bearing"). The verse at the bottom is beautifully written: "In Winter or Summer, sunshine or rain, whether it be noontide or midnight, somewhere the sun beats down on the new turned furrow of a John Deere Plow and from its polished moldboard reflects the glory of its maker." The phrase "The Sun Never Sets on a John Deere Plow" is in between the deer's antlers. Beautiful in its own right, this charming collectible can be reasonably valued between $1,000 and $3,000, depending on its condition. *Nick Cedar*

While some would complain that John Deere equipment is expensive, others would say it helps them save money. For the latter, John Deere promotional wallets, billfolds, and coin banks are ideal places to keep their extra dough. Collectors find it rather ironic that they have to pay a pretty penny for something called a "Titewad," which is an early billfold design that folded into a tiny rectangle. Coin banks of several varieties existed, although none are quite as famous as the "blacksmith" bank model. Another popular bank is the oil can issued for Deere's centennial celebration. Even paper money has been printed by the company as part of various promotional efforts.

This assortment of wallets shows the variety of leather goods bearing the John Deere name and trademark. The leather liplike coin purse (lower left) is stamped with the words "Bottineau Implement Co. John Deere." The upper right wallet is a "postal card" printed on soft suede-like leather. A United States of America seal and 1-cent McKinley postage stamp flank the upper corners. The actual postmark comes from "Moline, Ill. Dec. 18, 7 PM, 1905." The handwritten address directs the mail to "Mr. Charles H. Deere, Moline, Ill." The unique piece opens up to include a place to put money, receipts, and other paperwork. The billfold (lower right) is a simpler design with an imprint of the four-legged deer and a crawler tractor. Given its unique featured product, this piece is particularly difficult to find. The other three wallets with their narrow folded design are called "Titewads." The dark brown ones feature the bust of John Deere on the outer cover. The inside of one was stamped "John Deere Harvester Works" while others are found blank or imprinted with a different factory. The upper wallet of lighter brown leather is imprinted with an aerial view of the "John Deere Plow Works. Largest in the World." The "Titewad" imprint states it was "patented Nov. 29, 1909." These wallets are shown as an available John Deere souvenir as early as 1916. A 1930 catalog said, "The John Deere TiteWad bill fold for new-sized currency . . . is an exceptionally high-grade souvenir made of the best calf-skin. It is a possession any customer will prize. Price 30 cents each, plus postage." By 1940, dealers were able to buy these for 55 cents each. *Nick Cedar*

This trio of banks shows the hero as John Deere, the blacksmith. His right arm holds a hammer, which pounds the coin into the anvil when a spring-loaded button at the rear is depressed. This mechanical bank is designed in the tradition of the antique penny banks that were so popular in the 1800s. Yet these John Deere designs are nowhere near that old. A couple of major variations exist—mostly reproductions recently reissued by John Deere or fakes sold by unauthorized wholesalers. All three banks measure approximately 9 inches tall, but the one on the left is the crudest from a workmanship and detail standpoint. It's also the heaviest, weighing 5 pounds. Made of cast iron, this version says "Bank" on one side of the base and "Bank on John Deere Quality" on the front. The other two versions (gold plated and painted plastic) were reproduced for the John Deere Expo 1994/New Orleans Aftermarket 2000. According to Deere, the crude version was the result of an almost-run promotion involving door prizes for the 1977 Farming Frontiers John Deere Day shows. An informed source reports that the order for 18,000 banks to be made in Taiwan was cancelled after top management decided the design was inferior in quality and did not match the approved prototype. Production ceased and all tooling was supposed to have been destroyed. By 1984, Deere discovered a New Jersey wholesaler illegally selling reproductions as antique cast-iron banks. *Nick Cedar*

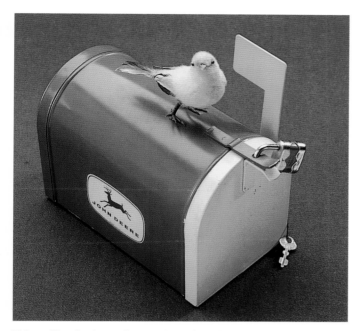

This mailbox bank was first used as a John Deere promotion during the 1960s. The four-legged deer decal shown here was later replaced by a two-legged design to match a trademark update. Measuring 6 inches in length, these metal mailboxes produced in 1966 are green with yellow doors and a metal flag. A yellow finch perches atop the metal mailbox. In 1984, a new version was introduced with a plastic flag and decal on the front. In 1990, John Deere released another style of bank with molded stripes in the box and a larger stickerlike decal. The coin slot is on the top of the newest variation, compared to its location at the back of the earlier banks. All four types of mailbox banks include a small padlock and set of keys. Some versions allowed for personalization with a set of stick-on letters. For the original versions, prices range from $100 for one in good condition (with bird) to $300 new in the box. Recent editions can be found for $25 or less. *Nick Cedar*

Dealers once gave away wooden nickels imprinted with advertising messages like these three coins that promote the General Purpose (GP) tractor, manure spreader, and heavy-duty farm wagon. Each nickel has a three-legged, leaping-deer logo that best matches the 1912 trademark. Judging from the products featured, these pseudo-coins are newer than that. For example, the GP tractor was introduced in 1928 and made until 1935. The vertical right-hand exhaust and left-hand air cleaner denote that this was the large-bore "X/O crossover" model built from 1930 to 1935. The manure spreader is the Model E, "The Original Low Down Spreader," introduced in 1932. Note the early design with a seat at the front where a lucky driver would sit during this unpleasant chore. The farm wagon appears to be a "Triumph" model first built in 1914. Deere built wood wagons until 1947. Given the low-quality painting process, the smudged ink makes these tokens look rather rough and possibly raises some doubts about authenticity. *Nick Cedar*

This $25 bill will certainly make you look twice. Instead of a bust from a hallowed leader of the United States, the famed stag deer positioned inside the large letter "D" steals the limelight on this bill made by the American Bank Note Company. Printed and issued in 1979 as part of a promotional effort, this money "can be exchanged at face value for goods and services at any John Deere agricultural dealership when properly endorsed by the registered owner." Rumored to have been discontinued, recalled, and destroyed due to counterfeiting claims, John Deere money found today could be worth much more than its face value to interested collectors. Other denominations are known to exist. *Nick Cedar*

The metal edging and paper-thin red cloth interior of this pretty pearl coin purse give the impression of age, probably around the 1920s. However, the plow pin attached to it may not be part of the original design. Perhaps not created intentionally to fool collectors, even a rough reproduction can cause a collector to part with big bucks for no good reason. *Nick Cedar*

True John Deere fanatics who list green as their favorite color can usually be found wearing something with a leaping-deer logo. Whether it's a cap, jacket, work boots, or even bright green suspenders, John Deere enthusiasts are proud to exhibit their brand loyalty. Over the years, John Deere has stitched its name on millions of caps, shirts, sweaters, sweatshirts, coats, jackets, even aprons. Companies like K-Products, Swingster, and American Identity made many of these "wearables" for John Deere over the years.

Due to the sheer number of company-related clothing items, these are not that valuable as a collectible today. However, this logo-adorned clothing still represents an intense loyalty to the John Deere brand. Perhaps the most interesting pieces of clothing memorabilia come from within the company itself—such as a uniform, hardhat, or other company-issued item.

Offered to dealers as an advertising specialty, this white sun helmet looks more like a hardhat one might wear on a safari to the jungle. Sporting the Quality Farm Equipment logo, this stylish hardhat is made of water-resistant papier-mâché. Also known as a pith helmet, a hat like this in good shape might bring $50 on the collectible market. *Nick Cedar*

This clothing patch best resembles the 1936 trademark design. While this may look like a homemade handicraft, it was actually part of a dealerships' coveralls. *Denny Eilers*

It's unlikely that Dr. Seuss had John Deere in mind when he started writing the book *Green Eggs and Ham*. Yet Deere & Company's promotional items were just as popular in the kitchen as they were in the garage. Deere catered to "women-folk" with an assortment of handy household devices, such as dispensers, serving utensils, and other convenient tools of the trade—everything from refrigerator magnets and ice cream scoops to toothpick holders and waxed-paper dispensers.

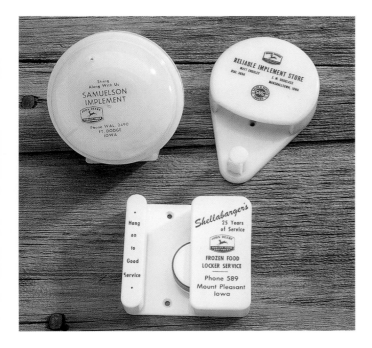

Handy household dispensers proved to be popular promotional items in the 1940s and 1950s. Dealers emblazoned their namesake, phone number, and slogan on a myriad of kitchen gadgets, including the string holder, tape dispenser, and broom holder shown here. These pearl-white plastic pieces sport catchy phrases like "String Along With Us" and "Hang on to Good Service." *Nick Cedar*

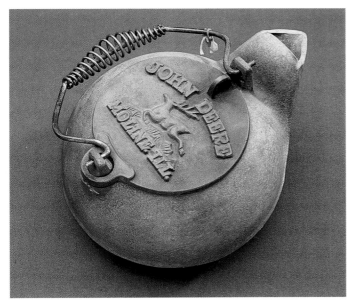

An unusual antique tea kettle made of cast iron uses a small lid similar to an early John Deere planter lid. The story behind this kettle is somewhat shrouded in mystery, although some believe they were giveaways out of the Kansas City branch. However, these pots could also have been handmade by an industrious employee or creative collector. Apparently, other variations exist, including ones that say "Made in Taiwan," so take care to research any antique kettle claiming to be "genuine" John Deere. *Nick Cedar*

Not exactly considered an everyday tool by today's standards, bottle openers were a must-have before screw-off tops found their way onto beverage bottles. This 1950s–1960s opener from Manson Implement in Iowa includes two plastic tops to keep the "fizz" in opened bottles of soda. *Nick Cedar*

Another common promotional item is the display plate, although these are believed to be actual dining dishes. The top plate from the "John Deere Plow Co. of Kansas City" has the four-legged deer leaping over the six-state territory of the Kansas City branch. The bottom plate is another branch-specific version from the Deere & Webber Company, the Minneapolis branch office. The Quality Farm Equipment logo shoots stars to key locations within the states of Deere & Webber territory. Rumored to have been used in the cafeteria/dining hall of the branch office or warehouse, the bottom plate actually has cutlery marks on its face. *Nick Cedar*

This large serving plate once belonged to Mrs. William Hewitt, who supposedly brought it back as a souvenir from a trip to Europe in the 1950s. Her husband served as the sixth president of Deere & Company from 1955 to 1982. Measuring 18 inches in diameter, the plate is beautifully decorated with colorful flowers along the outer rim. In the center is a collage of various pieces of farm equipment with a steel plow at the center. Next to this artwork is a woman tending to a butter churn and a man raising his glass. A banner declaring "God Speed the Plough" flies at their feet. Below this is an idyllic pasture scene with happy horses, chickens, pigs, and a cow. The bottom center area contains a beautifully worded verse about farming. The paragraph reads: "Let the wealthy and great roll in splendour and state. I envy them not. I declare it. I eat my lamb, my own chickens and ham. I shear my fleece and I wear it. I have lawns. I have bowers. I have fruits. I have flowers. The lark is my morning alarmer. So jolly boys here now here's God speed the plough. Long life and success to the farmer." The banner below says "Industry Produceth Wealth." While this plate says nothing of John Deere specifically, the fact that it was owned by Mrs. Hewitt makes it an interesting collectible. What's more, the nice verse about agriculture adds to its decorative appeal. *Nick Cedar*

Some diehard American collectors show no interest in international items from Deere & Company. Others find this piece of Deere's history highly interesting and seek out the items and stories that accompany the pieces. Many are related to overseas factories or companies Deere acquired, such as Lanz, a German tractor manufacturer. Others are promotional items from overseas dealers and international divisions. No matter what the intent, international items broaden the horizons for John Deere collectors looking for a special piece of company history.

These two pewter medallions marked "22 August 1967" and "Serie [sic] 20" were likely part of a giveaway when the 20 Series tractors were introduced overseas. Built at the Mannheim, Germany, factory, eight models made their debut in Europe with full fenders, left-hand passenger seat, locally required lighting, and optional four-post ROPS or outside suppliers' cabs. *Nick Cedar*

This unique assortment of international items highlights the worldwide recognition of the John Deere brand. From a factory in France to Caracas, Venezuela, and even Jamaica, John Deere promotional items are not limited to the shores of the United States. The three silver pieces in the bottom row (change tray, bottle opener, key chain) mark the 1-millionth engine built by the Saran, France, factory in 1993. The gold flip-top calendar displays a Model 50 or 60 tractor on the front and says, "C.ADE TRACTORES Y MAQUINARIAS CARACAS LA ENCRUCIJADA BARQUISIMETO" on the back. This Spanish piece comes from Caracas, Venezuela. The upper right pen-holder is also a thermometer made by Honeywell. Complete with the four-legged deer logo, the base states "Conferencia John Deere. Jamaica. Agosto 1966." *Nick Cedar*

Collectors can choose from a smorgasbord of John Deere memorabilia! Pens, pins, and plows are just a few of the "unique antiques" on the market today. Items shown include The Operation, Care, and Repair of Farm Machinery book (28th edition), straw children's hat with 1950 logo, "Leaping Lager Team Deere Beer" bottle, anvil paperweight on wood base with quote, 10-inch walking plow replica, plastic dual salt-pepper shaker with Minnesota dealer imprint, 150th anniversary matchbox, Velie/Deere letter opener, John Deere Plow Co. Kansas City clutch pin for "Up-to-Date" saddles, collars, and harness, employee service award money clip, oil can charm, pearlized ballpoint pen with Studebaker logo, Kemp & Burpee manure spreader spinner fob, Waterloo Boy colored button, and a John Deere Tractor Co. Waterloo, Iowa bullet lighter. *Nick Cedar*

CHAPTER 3

Catchall: Unique Antiques

Any time you're dealing with a company that's been around for more than 160 years, employed an estimated 1 million people, and sold products in more than 160 countries around the world . . . you're bound to have a pile of leftovers even after neatly organizing everything into categories. The Catchall chapter is the perfect place for all those things that fall between the cracks. This includes collectibles related to employees, dealers, factories, branches, awards, anniversaries, activities, events, Moline, and connected companies. Believe it or not, there are still items that escape classification! These miscellaneous matters and extra "whatchamacallits" are amusing, amazing, and even aptly named. In any case, these unique collectibles offer additional insight into the history of John Deere.

Personnel Perks

For many, working within the Deere & Company organization comes with a certain level of prestige and honor. Employees also receive an added list of benefits, including internal access to anything and everything Deere—from pens and paper to caps and clothing, even work badges and service awards!

The practice of awarding employees for service to the company began in 1925 when William Butterworth (1864–1936), Deere's CEO from 1907 to 1928, proposed the following policy: "The Officers and Directors of this Company feel that they would like to recognize long and continuous service and while we cannot express, by a button, the great appreciation that we feel for the service and loyalty of those who will receive them, still it is a badge which symbolizes the sincere recognition which we wish to give to this splendid service. In distributing these buttons, we hope that it will be done with some kind of ceremony, which will indicate to those receiving them, our sincere appreciation of their service."

Since that announcement, active employees have earned service awards in five-year increments. A retiree also receives a pin marking the years of employment with Deere & Company. On the back of the pin, an engraving of the retiree's initials and years of service further distinguishes a retiree award from an active employee service award. A jewel system (see page 42) designates the years of service for both of these awards.

Over the 75 years of this practice, only two designs of service pins are known to exist—both with the bust of John Deere. The original design is oval-shaped with the words "John Deere" and the years of service stamped on it. In 1975, a newer design made its debut as a round, gold-rimmed pin. Today, employees are offered a broad choice of 10-karat gold jewelry ranging from the traditional lapel pin to a tie bar, necklace, bracelet, ring, cuff links, money clip, watch, and other items. According to Human Resources, Deere & Company currently offers employees a choice of an estimated 25 items, depending on the employee's years of service with the company.

As decreed by CEO William Butterworth in 1925, an official ceremony marks the process of awarding service pins to employees. Two styles of these pins exist, and they both feature the bust of John Deere. The years of service are noted on the older style, and stones designate this number on the current style. *Nick Cedar*

John Deere Service Awards

When active employees of Deere & Company receive service awards, the awards are embellished as follows:

5-year = no jewel
10-year = 1 emerald
15-year = 2 emeralds
20-year = 3 emeralds
25-year = 1 diamond
30-year = 2 emeralds & 1 diamond
35-year = 2 diamonds & 1 emerald
40-year = 3 diamonds
45-year = 4 diamonds
50-year = 5 diamonds

Retired employees of Deere & Company receive service awards that are decorated as follows:

1 to 20 years = 1 diamond
20 to 29 years = 2 diamonds
30 to 39 years = 3 diamonds
40 to 49 years = 4 diamonds
50-plus years = 5 diamonds

Above left: Given to employees for service awards or to celebrate retirement, this attractive 10-karat gold jewelry dresses up any occasion. From rings and necklaces to watches, cuff links, money clips, and tie bars, a piece of this jewelry serves as a reminder of an employee's career with Deere. *Nick Cedar*

Above: These work badges identified employees for admittance into the factory or office during the 1940s. Other types of badges include security, police, fire, and chauffeur. Former employees report that the colors identified a particular shift, floor, or area of the plant. *Nick Cedar*

Work badges were used in the 1940s to identify employees for admittance into the factory or office. A few variations in design can be found. Some have a shield-type shape with the four-legged deer logo surrounded by the location name with a number underneath. Colors identified a particular shift or area of the plant. Another design is a smaller, simpler pin with the bust of John Deere on it. And a third design doesn't even have a logo; it's simply a round pin with the name of the plant and a number. These pin-type badges gave way to laminated photo-ID cards in the 1960s. Today, most factories and offices use computer-coded cards for employee identification.

Employees also received special Christmas gifts, such as this manicure set given to William M. Kaplan in 1938, compliments of the John Deere Plow Company, Kansas City, Missouri. A brush, clippers, nail file, and comb were included in the set. *Nick Cedar*

This green metal mailbox once held repair orders at "Turner Implement Co. Williamston, Mich., Phone: 471." The four-legged deer decal dates this piece between 1956 and 1968. *Nick Cedar*

This large metal box served as a dealer's prospect file drawer (ca. 1950s). Dealers could track customer information on index cards. By knowing the age and type of equipment a customer currently owned, a dealer could target new products to a customer in need. The card system helped dealers track what equipment was sold to which customer. Prospect books and binders are also popular collectibles dating way back to the 1910s. *Nick Cedar*

With more than 1,600 locations in North America alone, the John Deere dealer network covers the agricultural market with a wide-reaching web of local retail outlets. As distributors of the famed equipment, John Deere dealers often earn special perks and prizes for their role within the company organization. Naturally, Deere gives its dealers special materials for marketing and promoting the equipment to local customers. Deere also provides its dealers with necessary equipment to run a sales operation—from prospect drawers to dealership displays.

Dealers receive special treatment when they are privy to new product information prior to product launch. Deere & Company hosts annual meetings to introduce the new products to its dealers and sales force before announcing the innovations to the public. For instance, many special items are produced to excite dealers about the new

equipment at these product launches. Collectors have discovered these "limited edition" collectibles that were presented only to John Deere dealers.

Today, just about everything associated with a John Deere dealership is considered a collectible. That includes store signage, product displays, promotional items, ledger books, shop tools, manuals, parts drawers, and all marketing materials. Many collectors are partial to memorabilia from a dealership in their area, even if that dealer changed names or went out of business. As a direct result of their interest in the brand and access to company items, many retired dealers and dealership employees are prolific collectors of John Deere memorabilia today.

For the first 30 years of its business life, Deere & Company was a highly centralized organization based out of Moline. Sales personnel known as "travelers" sold John Deere products all over the country. However, these independent individuals out in the field had very little loyalty to Deere. Charles Deere decided to organize the first separate sales branch of the John Deere Plow Company at Kansas City, Missouri, in 1869. The co-partnership was named Deere, Mansur & Company. Between 1869 and 1889, Deere added four more sales branches in cities across the country—St. Louis, Missouri (Mansur & Tebbets Implement Company); Minneapolis, Minnesota (Deere & Webber Company); Council Bluffs, Iowa/Omaha, Nebraska (Deere, Wells & Company); and San Francisco, California (Marcus C. Hawley & Company).

As the nation's population began to spread out geographically, so did Deere's development of branch houses. Today, Deere's agricultural division involves 10 sales branches in North America, including several of the original cities: Atlanta, Georgia; Columbus, Ohio; Dallas, Texas; Davenport, Iowa; Grimsby, Ontario, Canada; Lenexa, Kansas; Moline, Illinois; Kansas City, Missouri; Minneapolis, Minnesota; and Reno, Nevada. Some of these locations are considered regional offices rather than full-fledged branches. As a global company, Deere also supports 11 overseas branches in China, Australia, Spain, Germany, Italy, Mexico, Uruguay, South Africa, England, France, and Argentina.

Over the years, these branch houses often issued their own promotional materials, only adding to the market for John Deere memorabilia. Sometimes, certain products were sold exclusively at a specific branch, making these items attractive finds for collectors. One such example is the Lindeman Crawler track-type tractor, sold primarily from the Portland, Oregon, branch.

The 1886 general catalog and envelope are from Deere, Mansur & Company of Kansas City, Missouri, which became the first sales branch of the John Deere Plow Company in 1869. This branch apparently sold saddles, collars, and harnesses in the late 1880s. Some collectibles (right) can be found with the "Up-To-Date" slogan and a logo of a deer's head inside a large letter "D." Often confused with the Kansas City branch, the Deere & Mansur Company (see orange pocket folder) started building corn planters in 1877. Until 1909, Deere & Mansur was a wholly separate company, but sold its planters under the Deere label through Deere branch houses, including the Deere, Mansur & Company in Kansas City. *Nick Cedar*

Deere & Webber, The Minneapolis Branch

One of the more active branches in the Deere organization, Deere & Webber can be credited with selling the famous wooden-wheeled Deere bicycles in the late 1890s. It also sold wagons and buggies, yet manager Charles C. Webber warned the company about spreading itself too thin. He said, "There is one thing that you should not allow your travelers to forget . . . that is, that their first duty is to get the plow trade, that that is the main business as long as they are connected with a Deere house. . . . In the hustle for wagon trade, buggy trade, and trade in general, none of us want to overlook the fact that plow trade is our principal mission."

C. C. Webber, a grandson of John Deere, became the manager of the Minneapolis branch in 1881. He also served on the board of directors from 1886 to 1944. Webber was the instigator for Deere to develop a small two- or three-plow tractor that would sell for about $700 in 1914. The Dain All-Wheel Drive was developed between 1915 and 1917 as a result. In October 1944, Webber died at the age of 85, after serving an unprecedented 67 years with Deere & Company. For 58 years, he was directly involved in general management of the company, significantly influencing the organization and its product line. In fact, his peers designated him "the dean of the American implement industry."

The 1901 *Farmer's Pocket Companion*, matchsafe, carriage tag, and 1930 product catalog represent the influence of Deere & Webber Company, the Minneapolis branch of Deere & Company. *Nick Cedar*

Just as the branch would put out its own specialized materials on occasion, a John Deere factory would also produce its own commemorative collectibles to mark certain events. These items have now become fair game for John Deere collectors interested in owning these types of "internal" memorabilia. In more than 160 years, John Deere manufacturing has come a long way since the first steel plow was forged in a blacksmith's shop in Grand Detour, Illinois.

A 1929 general catalog summarizes the success of John Deere's plow business: "From the three plows made by John Deere at a single forge in 1837 to the many thousands of plows and kindred tools now made by the John Deere Plow Works in a year is a stupendous jump. All the world knows how this factory has continued to grow to its present proportions at Moline, Illinois. It is the largest steel-plow factory in the world, with a floor space equal to a 40-acre farm, employing a large force of men, many of whom are skilled workmen who have spent a lifetime in making plows better."

Today, John Deere equipment is built at 23 factories in the United States and abroad. Through joint ventures and partnerships, factories in France, Germany, Brazil, the Netherlands, China, Mexico, South Africa, Argentina, and Canada join seven U.S. plants in manufacturing the famous brand of agricultural equipment.

The Des Moines, Iowa, plant (Des Moines Works) makes cotton harvesting, tillage, and planting equipment. The East Moline/Silvis, Illinois, factory (Harvester Works) builds combine harvesters and serves as an engineering center. Planting equipment and hydraulic cylinders also come from a factory in Moline, Illinois; and the Ottumwa, Iowa, factory produces hay and forage equipment. The Waterloo, Iowa, factory (Waterloo Tractor Works) builds agricultural tractors and major components, and also serves as an engineering center and foundry. A plant in Thibodaux, Louisiana, makes sugarcane harvesters and spraying equipment; and the Valley City, North Dakota, factory builds air seeding equipment.

At the end of World War II, Deere & Company operated 16 manufacturing facilities:

- John Deere Plow Works—Moline, Illinois: Cultivators, bedders, listers, and disk tillers.
- Wagon Works—Moline, Illinois: Farm wagons, rotary hoes, stalk cutters, and other products.
- Planter Works—Moline, Illinois: Corn planters, cotton planters, and disk harrows.
- Harvester Works—East Moline, Illinois: Combines, mowers, threshers, binders, pickers, and windrowers.
- Spreader Works—East Moline, Illinois: Manure spreaders, corn shellers, cotton harvesters, and grain elevators.
- Waterloo Tractor Works—Waterloo, Iowa: Farm tractors (gasoline and diesel) and large stationary engines.
- Dubuque Tractor Works—Dubuque, Iowa: Farm tractors (general-purpose and track-type) and small stationary engines.
- Des Moines Works—Des Moines, Iowa: Corn pickers, row-crop cultivators, and cotton pickers.
- Ottumwa Works—Ottumwa, Iowa: Hay rakes, balers, choppers, and forage blowers.
- Van Brunt Works—Horicon, Wisconsin: Grain drills, lime and fertilizer distributors, integral and drawn field cultivators.
- Killefer Works—Los Angeles, California: Deep-tillage tools, harrows, land levelers, and tool carriers.
- Yakima Works—Yakima, Washington: Tool carriers and attachments such as plows, harrows, and transplanters.
- Syracuse Chilled Plow Works—Syracuse, New York: Chilled plow bottoms and shares, harrows, potato machinery, and snow plows.
- Welland Works—Welland, Ontario, Canada: Grain and corn binders, disk tillers, seeding attachments, field cultivators, and grain drills.
- Union Malleable Iron Works—East Moline, Illinois: Malleable castings for associated factories.
- Vermilion Malleable Works—Hoopeston, Illinois: Malleable castings for associated factories.

Other Company Connections

One might assume that only Deere-branded items are collectible. That is certainly not the case, however, as memorabilia from *any* related company or business connected with Deere is also highly sought. In some cases, Deere acquired these companies, or marketed their products through Deere dealerships.

Deere & Company added a number of companies to the fold in order to grow its business and expand its product line. Many of these companies were separate entities with established brands before John Deere purchased

To mark the opening of the John Deere foundry in Waterloo, Iowa, this "First Iron" paperweight was created in September 1972. *Nick Cedar*

them. In fact, many of these product lines were actually marketed by John Deere sales branches prior to being bought by Deere.

The biggest acquisition era involved the purchase of 14 companies between 1900 and 1912. On January 6, 1910, the board of directors passed a resolution outlining a plan to reorganize the company by consolidating the branch houses, Union Malleable, Deere & Mansur, plus several separate companies under one new identity to be called Deere & Company.

A colorful trading card and piece of letterhead (1905) from Minneapolis branch Deere & Webber touts this fact: "Good wood, thoroughly well seasoned, is the foundation for a good wagon." Wheelwright James First, who was once a blacksmith for John Deere, founded the Moline Wagon Company in 1854. He partnered with Morris Rosenfield and Charles Benser in 1869. As president in 1881, Rosenfield invested in Deere, Wells & Company, a John Deere sales branch in Omaha. Soon other Deere branches were also selling "The Moline" wagon to the point that more than 1 million were in use by 1909. A year later, Deere bought the business and renamed it the John Deere Wagon Company. In 1913, it became the Wagon Works. *Nick Cedar*

Sold by the Minneapolis branch, the Sharples Cream Separator is promoted on this piece of 1904 letterhead as the "Easiest to Clean. Closest Skimmer." A cello pinback button says the tubular cream separator is "Different from the Others." And the pocket booklet with rhyming story about "week-day sense" further advertises these products from the Sharples Company of Chicago. *Nick Cedar*

Van Brunt Manufacturing gave John Deere its line of grain drills from 1911 to 1970, when production was transferred to the Des Moines Works. The large item on the right is the end of a seed box. The stamped-metal pieces simulating ashtrays are inscribed with "John Deere," the leaping-over-the-log trademark, and these words: "Sample of Material Used in John Deere Van Brunt Steel Box Drills." The other item is an employee badge. *Nick Cedar*

This button-sized mirror comes from the Fort Smith Wagon Company, one of Deere's primary wagon suppliers by 1905. The company first began in Indiana as the South Bend Wagon Company but moved to Fort Smith, Arkansas, in 1904. The slogan "From Forest to Farm" was associated with these wooden wagons because the factory was surrounded by thousands of acres of oak, ash, and hickory trees right in the heart of Arkansas' hardwood timber country. John Deere's sales branches took over in May 1907, and the company became an official part of the Deere & Company organization in 1910. Wagon production moved to Moline in 1925. *Nick Cedar*

The Union Malleable Iron Company was a supplier of malleable castings to John Deere as early as the 1870s. Deere acquired the foundry by 1911. Rumored to have made horseshoes in the past, the large brass one ("2LB8OZ") and the smaller paperweight version may authenticate the story. One possible version says that the pitching shoes were made for a special purpose such as a company picnic. It's not known what the wrench was used for, as the foundry didn't make implements itself. The circular paperweight (upper right) features the bust of William McKinley, president of the United States from 1897 to 1901. The Oriental lady change tray remains a mystery as to its origin and purpose. *Nick Cedar*

An 1897 catalog, colorful trading cards, postcard, and watch fobs hail from the Syracuse Chilled Plow Company of Syracuse, New York, which was established in 1879. The company joined the Deere organization in the early 1900s, adding a popular chilled-plow design to the John Deere product line. *Nick Cedar*

As shown on this piece of letterhead from Deere & Webber in 1905, Deere sold the famed "Success" manure spreaders from the Kemp & Burpee Manufacturing Company of Syracuse, New York. The small spinner fob and brass fob on a black ribbon also promote these manure spreaders. In late 1910, the company joined John Deere and the operation moved to East Moline. *Nick Cedar*

Kemp & Burpee of Syracuse, New York, made a manure spreader marketed by John Deere in the early 1900s. These promotional items (change tray, fobs, and pin holders) use the lion image to promote the company's "Success" line of manure spreaders. *Nick Cedar*

Velie Vehicles

The Velie name became a part of the Deere dynasty in 1860 when John Deere's daughter, Emma, married Stephen H. Velie. In 1863, Velie joined his father-in-law and brother-in-law at the John Deere Plow Works. As a close friend and confidant to Charles Deere, Velie served as secretary/chief financial officer, helping develop the plow business until his death in 1895. Velie's three sons, Charles Deere Velie, Stephen H., Jr., and Willard L., eventually went to work for the Deere organization. In 1902, Willard launched the Velie Carriage Company to manufacture a full line of buggies, carriages, surreys, driving wagons, and spring wagons called the "Wrought Iron Line" of vehicles. As automobiles gained popularity, the buggy business waned until it was phased out around 1919.

In 1908, the Velie Motor Vehicle Co. incorporated and began manufacturing automobiles, which were marketed through the Deere dealer network. The Velie Motor Car Co. also existed briefly (1909–1912). Willard started the Velie Engineering Co. in 1911 to build gas, steam, and electric motors and engines, plus automobile accessories and motor trucks. In 1916, the Engineering Co. consolidated with the Motor Vehicle Co. to form the Velie Motors Corporation. Velie manufactured the "Biltwel" tractor from 1916 to 1920. The "Biltwel" name also represented a separate line of six-cylinder cars in 1916 and 1917. Oddly enough, Willard Velie helped push Deere to introduce a farm tractor during his term as director between 1911 and 1918. Experimental designs never succeeded, and Deere inherited the Waterloo Boy tractor line when it bought the Waterloo Gasoline Engine Company in 1918.

The Velie name was associated with carriages (Wrought Iron Vehicles) by 1902, motor trucks (Velie Engineering Company) in 1911, automobiles from 1908 to 1928, and tractors between 1916 and 1920. Willard Velie, Jr., even orchestrated a one-year stint building Monocoupe airplanes in 1928. Velie Motor Corp. produced 250,000 to 300,000 vehicles during the two decades the factory was in business.

A picture postcard featuring a Velie car "on the Old Santa Fe Trail" joins an assortment of other Velie-related memorabilia. A stick pin, watch fob, carriage tag, and pinback promote Velie cars and carriages. The letter opener has "Velie" on one side and "Deere" on the reverse (both sides shown). *Nick Cedar*

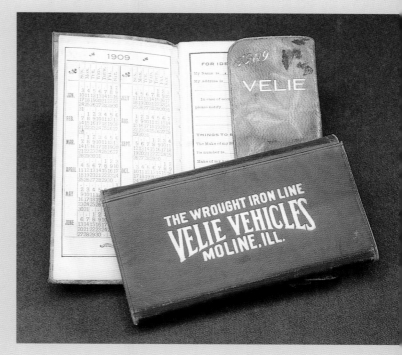

This brochure tells the adventures of the Velie car on its trip through the Grand Canyon. Photographs and colored images along with an excellent story line make this an interesting piece to include in any collection. The leather-bound pocket calendar, watch fob, and pinback reinforce that "The Name Insures the Quality" for "The Wrought Iron Line of Velie Vehicles, Moline, Ill." *Nick Cedar*

These two leather-bound calendars from Velie Vehicles date back to 1909 and 1915. This pair represents Velie's version of John Deere's famed "pocket companions," a popular promotional item in the late 1880s and early 1900s. *Nick Cedar*

Velie manufactured carriages and cars from 1902 to 1928. These pieces of literature elaborate on the specific product offerings in the line. The hubcaps come from a Velie vehicle, as does the radiator emblem. Note how that design is shown on the middle piece of literature. The medallion matches the logo used on the far right brochure. *Nick Cedar*

John Deere-Lanz

Heinrich Lanz built engines and threshers at his plant established in 1859 in Mannheim, Germany. On a visit to the United States in 1902, Lanz met John Deere's son, Charles. Heinrich's son, Karl, took over the business and later orchestrated a deal with the Deere organization. In 1911, Lanz built its first-style Landbau-Motor "field-working machine" and began to export models to Russia. However, the onset of World War I eliminated exports, so Lanz turned to wartime production of airships and airplanes.

After the war, Karl Lanz led the development of a new agricultural tractor, the legendary Bulldog, in 1921. Designed by Dr. Fritz Huber, the Bulldog was the world's first hot-bulb-fired, crude-oil-burning tractor. By World War II, Lanz had built more than 100,000 Bulldog tractors. At its peak, Lanz enjoyed more than 40 percent of all German tractor sales, with Deutz as the other prominent player. But World War II was a disaster for the company, as the majority of the Mannheim plant was leveled by Allied bombings in 1944 and 1945.

Still, the 200,000th Bulldog came off the line in 1956 when Deere purchased the Lanz line and factory. Two years later, the entire line of Bulldog blue-and-orange became John Deere green-and-yellow. By 1960, the first two models (300 and 500) of John Deere-Lanz tractors were introduced. Between 1962 and 1965, the 100 and 700 models joined the line. In 1966, the entire Mannheim line was updated as the 10 Series. In Germany, these models still carried the "John Deere-Lanz" nameplate, but the Lanz name was eventually dropped for other markets. There was also a Spanish line of Bulldogs from the Getafe, Spain, factory between 1956 and 1963. The Lanz Iberica line didn't get green paint until 1961. The first Deere-designed tractors rolled off the line in 1963. Today, the Mannheim factory still operates as a John Deere tractor plant.

The pair of red-and-yellow nameplates once adorned the grille of Lanz Bulldog models built between 1952 and 1960. The larger greenish Lanz nameplate matches ones on diesel models manufactured around 1960. The pewter pin (possibly a visitor's badge) shows the Mannheim factory with its famous water tower landmark that survived World War II bombing. The deck of playing cards says "Lanz. First Trump. Your bet is doubly safe with John Deere Lanz." *Denny Eilers*

The first John Deere-Lanz models came from the Mannheim, Germany, factory in 1960. The Lanz name was incorporated into the trademark leaping-deer logo as shown on some of these promotional items. A ballpoint pen, ornate pocketknife, tape measure, key chain, and Swiss Army knife advertise the German tractor manufacturer. *Nick Cedar*

Some say John Deere put Moline, Illinois, on the map. And there's certainly some truth to that. Since John Deere's decision in 1847 to move his plow business to the shores of the mighty Mississippi River, Moline has developed into a manufacturing mecca. John Deere purchased land and water rights near the new dam, where the new city of Moline began to grow. The famed "Quad Cities" nickname stuck as the four river towns of Moline (Illinois), Rock Island (Illinois), Davenport (Iowa), and Bettendorf (Iowa) became an attractive location for settlers and business developers alike.

In fact, the name "Moline" became synonymous with "plows" when Charles Deere was forced to sue a challenging hometown competitor. In 1867, Deere took Candee, Swan & Company to court for misrepresenting its plow as "the Moline Plow," which had become well known as Deere's own design. It was a landmark case in trademarks for the fact that it set the precedent about whether or not a company could claim "ownership" of a town's name after advertising it heavily.

The counterfeit company not only produced a nearly identical plow and deceptively advertised in similar fashion, but also copied the Deere trademark logo almost to the letter. By 1869, the court had ruled in Deere's favor, but an appeal resulted in an Illinois State Supreme Court review. The judge reversed the original decision in 1871, giving the Moline Plow Company the green light to continue competing with Deere and causing confusion with farmers.

This acclaimed enemy would drag Deere down again during a prolonged bid process in 1889 from a British syndicate who wanted to buy Deere & Company, Deere & Mansur, and the Moline Plow Company. Eventually, the deal fell through, but not before Charles Deere himself ended up owning shares of his competitor's stock. Later, Deere would compete with his rivals in plow (Flying Dutchman) and tractor (Moline Universal) manufacturing as well.

Employees also switched sides, leading to multiple clashes in court over design patents, branch battles, slanderous attacks, and the like. As it turns out, Deere seriously considered buying the Moline Plow Company's tractor plant in 1924, but it was sold to the International Harvester Company instead. The Moline Plow Company was then renamed the Moline Implement Company, which eventually consolidated into the Minneapolis-Moline business.

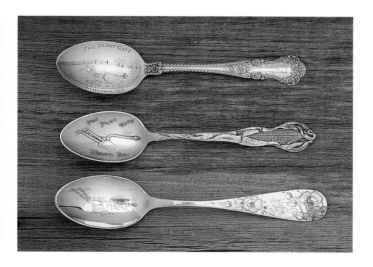

Above: A 1949 Illinois license plate and Moline centennial holder (1848–1948) is another example of memorabilia that is not directly Deere, but still an interesting collectible for diehard Deere fans. *Nick Cedar*

Above left : Moline earned the nickname of "Plow City" because of John Deere's famed invention. This generates an additional market of memorabilia for anything related to the city itself, home to the great Deere & Company since 1847. A name badge, ribbon, and watch fob tout the "Plow City" nickname. *Nick Cedar*

Left: It's doubtful anyone would say that John Deere was raised with a silver spoon in his mouth, but these beautiful silver spoons call Moline "The Plow City" and sport the celebrated plow he designed in 1837. The ornate inscriptions make this trio an attractive addition to any John Deere collection, let alone a spoon-specific one. While it can't be confirmed that Deere & Company actually produced any such items, some collectors couldn't care less—they'd be proud to own one of these commemorative spoons. *Nick Cedar*

In the course of its extensive history, Deere & Company has celebrated several significant milestones, won numerous awards, and been host to countless events and activities. Memorabilia associated with these awards, anniversaries, and activities are quite collectible today.

Since its beginnings in 1837, Deere & Company has commemorated its history in 25-year increments. Perhaps the most celebrated milestone was the centennial in 1937. Special items created to honor the 125th and 150th birthdays of the company also attract collectors today. Deere recently passed its 160th milestone and will celebrate its 175th year in business in 2012, which will no doubt generate a slew of special commemorative items in honor of the achievement. Unlike other major agricultural equipment manufacturers, Deere & Company has never been sold or merged with a competitor.

Deere plows continued to enter—and win—plowing contests all over the world. This beautiful silver trophy served as grand prize in the 1930 Wheatland Plowing Match. The John Deere Plow Company won the Manufacturers Class in this contest. Deere won a similar trophy for "1st prize" in 1928. *Denny Eilers*

This marble desk set marks the 125th anniversary in 1962. Given as a dealer award for tractor sales, this attractive piece made an impressive statement sitting on a dealer's desk in Mankato, Minnesota. *Nick Cedar*

Nicknamed the "Copper Pennies," this wall hanging was produced in 1937 for the centennial. The pair of 8-inch-diameter coins shows the two sides of the fobs, medallions, and coins created to commemorate Deere's 100th birthday. *Nick Cedar*

Deere commemorated its 150th anniversary celebration with a large number of specially marked souvenirs. A large display plate from the foundry, gold medallion, marble paperweight, glass paperweight, and button cover set show a sampling of the items involved with this milestone. *Nick Cedar*

In the early 1900s, Deere & Company held annual picnics for employees and their families at Campbell's Island on the Mississippi River in East Moline. These all-day events involved games and prizes, plus dinner and dancing.

On July 1, 1909, the *Tri-City News* ran the following story:

Moline, Ill., June 28—Employes [sic] of Deere & Co. and members of their families to a number of 14,607, enjoyed their annual outing on Campbell's Island last Thursday. There was a ball game in the afternoon, which a shop team won from the office force by a score of 6 to 0. The office force turned the tables on the shop men in a tug of war, winning contrary to the dope. A fine program of races and other athletic events provided the afternoon amusement and handsome prizes were awarded the winners. During the dinner and supper hours orchestra music was furnished, and afternoon and evening there was dancing. The company not only furnished prizes and free transportation to and from the island, but lemonade, coffee, cream and sugar were provided. It required 10,500 lemons to take care of the wants of the picknickers in the drinking line.

John Deere Day is an annual tradition. Since 1937, each John Deere dealership is host to a customer-appreciation event. Often held during the winter when farmers are not busy in the fields, these events draw large crowds of young and old. At most John Deere Days, the festivities include a meal and a show. The John Deere Day film both educates and entertains with human-interest stories as well as new product introductions. The star of this film is often a popular celebrity. Past hosts have included Walter Cronkite, Wilford Brimley, Richard Petty, Buster Keaton, and comedians Charlie Weaver and Andy Devine.

John Deere Day events serve as special promotional efforts in themselves. A theme or slogan usually accompanies each event and numerous promotional trinkets can be ordered with the theme, logo, and dealership imprint. From balloons and banners to pens and paper coffee cups, promotional paraphernalia for Deere Day spans the price range from mere pennies to big-ticket items.

 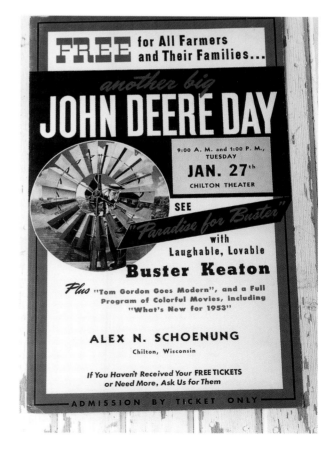

Posters played a primary part in the John Deere Day promotional effort. These colorful examples invite "all farmers and their families" to join in the free activities. In the early days, the company asked dealers to hand out tickets for admission. Today, that practice is no longer part of the John Deere Day event. Dealers often ordered custom-printed posters with their specific information on it. These two posters spread the word about John Deere Days in 1953 and 1955. *Michelle Schueder*

Above: Made from ruby-red glass, these ornate salt and pepper shakers once graced a table at a company picnic. An inscription reads: "Deere Picnic, July 20, 1907." According to former employees, Mrs. Charles Deere saw the special glass at the World's Fair and ordered several sets. Flat brass lids originally topped these shakers; these beautiful domed lids were added later. *Nick Cedar*

Above left: This ornate cream pitcher represents another ruby-red glass item specially made for the "Deere Picnic, July 20, 1907." *Denny Eilers*

Left: Another item from a company picnic, this delicate "ORDER" ribbon shows the bust of John Deere, the three-legged, leaping-over-the-log trademark, and the words: "Deere & Co. Twelfth Annual Picnic: 1913." *Denny Eilers*

So many items have held the Deere name or trademark logo that it's hard to fit them all into neat little categories. Therefore, this assortment of items includes medallions, paperweights, figurines, and other extra "whatchamacallits." In fact, you could probably fill an entire book with items that would be classified as "miscellaneous!" Still, some things simply defy classification. Many of these collectibles may surprise even the most seasoned collector. Other items will generate a few laughs. Either way, enjoy the diversity of these oddball, off-the-wall collectibles!

These Christmas ornaments are part of an annual series that started in 1996 and continues today. The 2-inch-diameter pewter medallions are hand painted with a particular winter scene involving a John Deere tractor. The first year depicts a Model D helping to harvest a Christmas tree. The 1997 edition shows two children and a dog frolicking in a snowball fight while dad pitches hay to the horses. The featured tractor is the Model L. According to collectors, the first edition is hard to find, making it worth around $300 today. More recent ornaments are readily available and priced appropriately. These small items that sell for around $12 brand-new won't break your collectible budget, and they make nice stocking stuffers for your favorite collector. *Nick Cedar*

The small brass dish (possibly a change tray) on the left shows the log-leaping deer "Trade Mark," a bust of "John Deere, Inventor of the Steel Plow," his famed creation, and the claim of "First Steel Plow." Experts estimate that this rare piece dates to around 1912. The item on the right is even more mysterious as to its purpose or origin. Seemingly a hanging tag of sorts, this cardboard shield-shaped cutout (ca. 1880s) shows three colored sections: red for the leaping deer, blue for the plow, and gold for the bust of John Deere with the words "John Deere. Manufacturer Pioneer of Steel Plows, Moline, Ill." The back of this tag also features three colored sections: blue with stars; red with a plow and ribbon; gold with a fireworks burst. The ribbon near the plow says "Shield of our Nation's Prosperity." *Nick Cedar*

This trio of gold calendar medallions represents a series that began in 1983 and still continues today with the year 2000 edition also shown. The bottom one displays the face of a typical medallion. This 1988 face shows the progression of official leaping-deer trademarks. *Nick Cedar*

This "Good Luck" token serves as the "membership emblem of the don't worry club." On the flip side it says "Waterloo Boy Gasoline Engines Are Sure to Bring You Good Luck. Waterloo, Iowa." Traditional good luck symbols are shown on the coin—a four-leaf clover, horseshoe, wishbone, and Plains Indian emblem. What looks like a swastika is actually a symbol called "twirling logs" that meant good luck to Native Americans. Another group considers it to be the "4-Ls" that stand for luck, light, love, and life. Experts note this "good" swastika is a reverse of the Nazi version. This rare token probably dates back to before Deere's purchase of the Waterloo Boy line in 1918. *Nick Cedar*

Nicknamed the "Maltese Cross," this is another example of an unusual paper piece. The front has red-and-blue triangles on a gold background with a plow and early leaping-over-log trademark. On the back, wording fills four sections plus a center area. Top: "This cross marks you a Knight of the Plow. Fasten the cord to your button." Right: "Established 1847. Incorporated 1868. The first slab of plow steel ever rolled in U.S. was made into JOHN DEERE PLOWS." Bottom: "WANTED: 100,000 farmers to send name and address on a postal [sic] for our FARMERS' POCKET COMPANION." Left: "If you want the best plow on earth see that it bears the TRADEMARK found on the other side." Center: "Our specialties: Gilpin Sulky Plow, Sylvan Cultivator, Deere Gang Plow, Deere Spring Cultivator, New Deal Wheeled Walking Plows." Because the first pocket companion was printed in 1879, that's the very earliest this piece could be dated. Yet the reference to the New Deal design comes from the mid-1880s when Deere adopted the three-wheeled plow approach. No matter what the exact date, top collectors estimate a value of around $200 for a Maltese Cross in good condition. *Nick Cedar*

As they say, art is subjective, which explains why this glass shadow box of green probably hung on the walls of more than one John Deere fan over the years. The styled Model A gives a clue as to its age—possibly as old as 1938. But upon closer inspection, note the armchair-type seat and electric lights, which were added to the Model A in early 1947. "Albert City Implement Co." of Albert City, Iowa, gave this piece "to our Deere friends & customers." *Brenda Kruse*

Given out when most sewing was done by hand, not by machine, promotional needle cases date back to the early 1900s. Note the stone at the end of the casing. The red one says "Velie Wrought Iron Vehicles" on one side and "John Deere Plows. The World's Standard" on the other. The white case uses blue lettering to say "John Deere Plow Co. Kansas City. Denver." on one side and "Quality is Remembered When Price is Forgotten" on the back. The white case actually contains a bullet pencil instead of needles. It's unclear whether it was originally a needle case or if the red one was originally a bullet pencil case. As one collector commented, "It's pretty fancy for a bullet pencil!" *Nick Cedar*

Aside from the deer, the walking plow is another symbol that is quickly and easily associated with John Deere. This 10-inch replica of the famed steel plow can be found in several variations. One is nicknamed the "FFA" version as it honored the Future Farmers of America. Others were possibly salesman incentive awards or dealer prizes. The John Deere name is cast into the handles. As with almost any collectible, values are higher if the piece comes with an original box. In this case, it's not that exciting, but it does add value—all for a plain cardboard box with a rare red oval sticker seal highlighting the 1912 logo. *Nick Cedar*

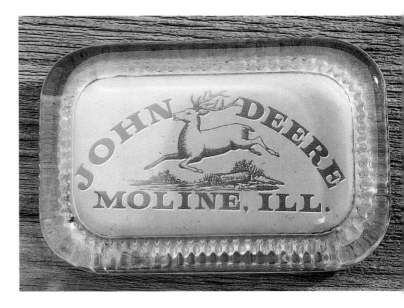

This rectangular glass paperweight holds the oldest leaping-log logo from 1876 on a maroon-colored insert. Although it does not appear to have been tampered with, supporting documentation does not exist to authenticate the piece. Still, many collectors believe this paperweight is legitimate. *Nick Cedar*

These beautiful brushes almost appear to be recent reproductions due to their unblemished, museum-quality condition. Patented in 1924, these clothes brushes were available to dealers as customer souvenirs. The large one measures 6 inches long and the round one is 3.5 inches in diameter. Either one makes an incredible addition to any collection. A 1930 specialty catalog caption under the round one says, "The brush is of extra quality and is easily and firmly held in the hand. The long fine bristles are set in hard Paravoid, which holds them securely and insures long life. Price, 25 cents each, plus postage." By 1940, the long one was featured and the price was up to 55 cents each. Today, collectors say $300–$700 is a reasonable range for either brush, but believe the long one is harder to find. *Nick Cedar*

There have been many deer figurines created over the 160-plus years of Deere's history. The larger brass figurine is actually a coin bank with the words "John Deere" stamped into the side of its body and "John Deere Plow Co. Moline, Ill." on the base. On the smaller brass paperweight (ca. 1926), the leaping-over-the-log deer is not trying to impersonate a unicorn . . . it's missing one rack—probably from an unintentional tumble to the floor. *Nick Cedar*

A night watchman or janitor at the "Administration Center" of Deere & Company in Moline is perhaps still missing this green and silver flashlight. Sporting a four-legged deer logo of 1956, it's the same design offered to dealers in a catalog of promotional items. *Nick Cedar*

This ornate gold piece is also somewhat of a mystery. The front says "John Deere Plow Co., 1903, Kansas City, Denver" with a four-legged deer leaping over the plow. The back says "The owner can be found by sending this to address on other side." In the center, a "No. 1903" further identifies this piece. It's unclear what this item was used for, as the hole appears to be drilled, not originally a cut-out part of the design. Some say a key fob; others a carriage tag. Only speculation and an educated guess can determine the origin of this treasured collectible. *Nick Cedar*

Left: In 1966, John Deere used a "Power Train" promotional tour to introduce the new 38- and 52-horsepower tractors—models 1020, 2020, and 2510. The album of railroad-themed songs, postcard, *The Furrow* magazine spread ad, model train, and coordinating First Aid and bug-repellant kits were part of this marketing ploy. *Nick Cedar*

Above: This beautiful gold tag promotes the "Reindeer Buggies" from the John Deere Plow Co. of Omaha, Nebraska, and Sioux Falls, South Dakota. Deere organized into five key branches between 1869 and 1889. The Omaha/Council Bluffs branch house opened in 1881, with Lucius Wells in charge of Deere, Wells & Company. The branch began in Council Bluffs, Iowa, but moved across the Missouri River to Omaha in 1899. The branch began to sell buggies in 1881 when the head of the Moline Wagon Company bought a one-third interest in the Deere co-partnership. During the 1880s and 1890s, the "Reindeer" name also stood for cultivators and bicycles. Driven by the advancements in the automobile industry, Deere's buggy business rode its way out of the product line and into the history books by 1921. *Denny Eilers*

These unique objects are somewhat of a mystery despite their popularity on the collectible market. Rumored to have once held matches, letters, or who knows what, these "whatchamacallits" could be as old as 1937 or as new as the 1990s due to unlicensed reproductions. Commonly considered letter-holders, several styles exist with details and differences to help determine which version is which. Collectors claim the originals have a rivet holding the pocket to the back, while the "repros" have a bolt/screw or are welded together. These cast-iron pieces, which are dated 1847 to mark the move to Moline, are painted gold in some cases, while others have bright green accents. *Nick Cedar*

With the growing market for anything Deere-related, items sporting a deer symbol or the familiar green-and-yellow paint often find their way onto a collector's shelf—even if they aren't genuine John Deere. For example, this prize was given as a joke from one collector to another. Although the words "John Deere" are nowhere to be found on the piece, its dual-deer stamped metal design makes it highly unusual—perhaps unique. Some say it looks like a fruit bowl; other, more "religious" collectors suggest it could be used as a Communion cup. Either way, it's sure to draw some attention . . . and probably even spawn a line of reproductions to be auctioned on the Internet! *Nick Cedar*

Not exactly "Near Beer," these bottles of "Team Deere Beer" became a bootlegged piece of memorabilia just a few years ago. Two kinds were bottled at a brewery in St. Louis, but quantities were extremely limited. While rumors abound about Deere entering the beer business, the truth behind these beers actually points back to the author! While working at an advertising agency on the John Deere account, the author and her "team" of coworkers ordered the beer from a local brewery and designed the special labels. Two versions of the beer were given as Christmas presents to the employees in the Ag Advertising department in 1995. Apparently a branch office ordered a couple cases of beer. But, Deere & Company did not approve, and the beer was confiscated and destroyed. As you can see, a few bottles survived . . . leaving an interesting collectible accompanied by an intriguing tale. *Nick Cedar*

Over its 160-plus-year history, Deere & Company left behind a paper trail of literature, ledgers, books and brochures as part of its collectible memorabilia. Items shown include a Quik-Tatch Cultivators brochure, Fertilizer Grain Drill brochure, plastic red taillight cover with Iowa dealer imprint, Farmer's Pocket Ledger Notebook (95th annual edition), 1/16-scale Eska-Carter Model K manure spreader, Deere & Webber Co. branch territory display plate, black desk set pen holder with 1956 logo, drinking glass with frosted 1937 logo, "New Way Air-Cooled" engine pocket mirror from KC branch, green Union Malleable Iron Works miniature horseshoe, Waterloo Tractor Works security badge, brushed chrome cigarette lighter with Oklahoma dealer imprint, celluloid pocket tape measure with 1950 logo, "Caterpillar" John Deere Day button, and a watch fob with colored celluloid inset of Model D tractor. *Nick Cedar*

CHAPTER 4

Ephemera:
Leaving a Paper Trail

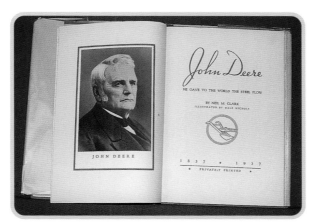

Just imagine how many pieces of paper have been created over the 160-plus years of Deere & Company history. Think about every piece of literature, letterhead, or ledger paper dealing with Deere's business as an equipment manufacturer . . . it's probably enough to make most environmentalists shudder.

Now consider the definition of ephemera: "items, such as pamphlets, notices, and tickets, originally intended to be of use for only a short time, especially when preserved as collectibles." When related to John Deere, that can mean anything that's on paper—from literature and letters, posters and postcards, to manuals, magazines, books, and brochures.

Some collectors specialize in paper products and have their file cabinets and bookshelves full of binders to prove it. Others are only interested in acquiring pieces of paper that supplement another item in their collection. For example, toy collectors may wish to own a copy of the literature featuring the full-size version of each tractor or implement in their scale-model collection. Restorers of antique equipment find the technical manuals of great help in putting all the parts and pieces back together again. In some cases, reprinted materials from Deere will suffice for their needs, but do not hold value like the vintage versions sought after by collectors.

A few collectors simply enjoy the historical aspects of collecting antique paper. Many business dealings in the past were accomplished in the form of letters between the two parties. This correspondence creates a paper trail that can be both educational and entertaining. Personal letters from Deere & Company executives are also collectible, as they connect a piece of paper to powerful people within the company.

Regardless of a collector's preference, the fact that century-old paper can still be found intact is quite a feat in itself. Considering how easy it is for paper to be thrown away, ripped or torn, dog-eared, written on, folded, crumpled, or otherwise mutilated, finding a near-perfect piece of paper from the 1800s and early 1900s is truly an impressive accomplishment.

Naturally, the condition of the paper plays a factor in its value as a collectible. However, even a heavily soiled piece may be worth more simply due to its age or rarity. As one collector put it, "Having one dirty copy is better than having none." Usually, collectors will then seek out a better copy of the piece and hope to sell the lower-quality one to another collector.

Fortunately, paper's prolific presence offers an easy starting place for new collectors. Most documents can be purchased for a relatively minor investment and, if properly protected in the years ahead, can show an increase in value accordingly. The following chapter highlights examples of the types of John Deere-related paper now considered collectible.

Privately printed in honor of Deere's centennial in 1937, this book written by Neil Clark told the story of John Deere's first 100 years in business. A copy autographed by Charles Deere Wiman and the board recently sold for $350 at an auction. *Brenda Kruse*

Deere & Company has not only issued numerous books and manuals; the company and its founder have also been the subject of several books as well. The most thorough coverage of Deere's history can be found in *John Deere's Company: A History of Deere & Company and its Times*, written in 1984 by Wayne Broehl. With more than 800 pages, this book provides a detailed review of John Deere's life and the growth of his blacksmith business into a global market leader as an equipment manufacturer.

An excerpt from Broehl's book best summarizes the impact of Deere's invention: "John Deere is an authentic American folk hero, whose legend began in his own lifetime when, in 1837, he developed a steel plow that cut without sticking through the rich prairie soil of the Midwest. Today, he is remembered as the person 'who gave to the world the steel plow.' . . . For many years the relationship between the farmer and the distinctive green Deere tractor in his field has been uniquely symbiotic."

Other books focus on the pioneer plowmaker, including one that chronicles the story of John Deere's first 100 years—*John Deere: He Gave To The World The Steel Plow*, written by Neil M. Clark in 1937. Numerous books have been published about the equipment, especially tractors. *The Big Book of John Deere Tractors*, by Don MacMillan

(1999) is one of the best books to cover all tractor models, and it also includes a sampling of collectible memorabilia, literature, and toys.

Since 1967, Deere's publishing division, John Deere Publishing, has been producing educational materials on a variety of ag-related topics. Nearly 50 books are available in the following series of guides—Farm Business Management, Fundamentals of Service, Fundamentals of Machine Operation, Fundamentals of Compact Equipment, and an Agricultural Primer Series. The subject matter of these books ranges from hydraulics and shop tools to soil management and tractors. Newer titles include high-tech topics such as computers, the Internet, and precision farming.

Another series called *The Operation, Care, and Repair of Farm Machinery* served a similar purpose in the past. Deere published 28 editions of these popular guides between 1927 and 1957. Four variations of cover designs are known to exist. The first 27 editions had simple cloth covers in blue, gray, or green. The final edition wore a cream-colored cover with green artwork of a tractor steering wheel in the firm grip of a farmer's hand.

Collectible values average $35 for most editions and range from $300 for the first one to $15 for the last one.

Johnny Tractor and his Pals, written by Louise Price Bell, and *Corny Cornpicker Finds a Home*, written by Lois Zortman Hobbs, have entertained little ones since 1958 and 1959. Illustrated by Roy A. Bostrom, these two children's books were reprinted in the late 1980s. *Nick Cedar*

These books contain quality information on operational, maintenance, and management procedures, but they mention no John Deere-specific models or equipment. Rather, these "generic" guides served as educational tools for high school and college students, farmers, do-it-yourselfers, repair technicians, and agribusiness professionals. Other helpful publications—and collectible items—include operator's manuals, parts catalogs, service bulletins, shop manuals, retail price lists, and other technical documentation that often accompanied a piece of equipment.

As a rule, every piece of John Deere equipment comes with an official operator's manual. This book served as an educational guide for operating the equipment, making appropriate adjustments, performing regular servicing, reordering parts, and other useful information on safety, specifications, troubleshooting tips, and other such matters. Early editions were simple black-and-white books; later versions had color covers and quality photography throughout the pages. Today, most operator's manuals come with a video supplement as well.

Unfortunately, these early reference books did not hold up well to the wear and tear of their ride in the toolbox. Some of the oldest manuals have virtually disintegrated from age. Deere eventually realized the protective value of durable covers, waterproof envelopes, and specific cubbyholes for storing these helpful guides.

In addition to books and manuals, John Deere also issued a number of magazines for its customers and employees. Perhaps the best-known publication is *The Furrow*, which made its debut in 1895 and is still printed today. Packed with advertising for John Deere products, *The Furrow* also highlights pertinent and timely topics about farming. Dealers pay to have the publication mailed to their customer list. Today, more than 31 versions of *The Furrow* are published in 12 languages and sent free to approximately 1.6 million subscribers in more than 40 countries worldwide.

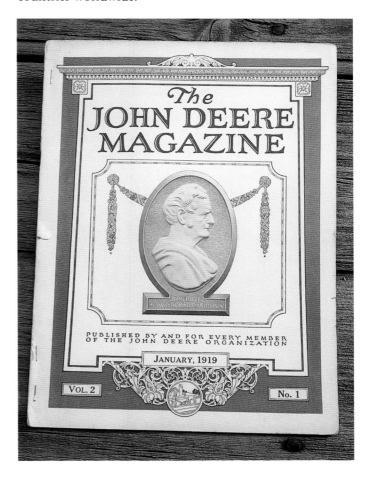

This edition of *The Furrow* magazine is one of the earliest. Dated "April, May, June 1897," this issue of "A Journal for the American Farmer" was "published quarterly by Oleson & Eveans, Ulen, Minn." A special feature article on Hindu farming in India and plowing with sacred oxen highlights this edition. There is also a section specifically for women readers. Products featured include Sharples cream separators, a Kentucky shoe drill, a John Deere bicycle, and Moline wagons. *Nick Cedar*

"Published by and for every member of the John Deere organization," *The John Deere Magazine* highlights information pertaining to employees of the John Deere organization. Articles on department activities, attendance, safety training, employee family news, and homes purchased on the John Deere Plan are covered in this issue from January 1919, Vol. 2, No. 1. In a 1921 edition, the duties of the president of the United States are listed, along with his salary of $75,000 per year. Today, a publication called the *JD Journal* performs a similar service by keeping employees and retirees informed of Deere's activities. *Nick Cedar*

John Deere issued an annual magazine for customers that featured Deere equipment, along with helpful advice on farming. For example, this 1909 issue of *Better Farming* magazine highlights John Deere plows, cultivators, gasoline engines, listers, and harrows. It also includes educational information on alfalfa and silage. Apparently, *Better Farming* was renamed *Modern Farming* for the 1954–1964 editions (1961 edition shown). Even today's collectors enjoy reading the helpful hints on production agriculture. *Nick Cedar*

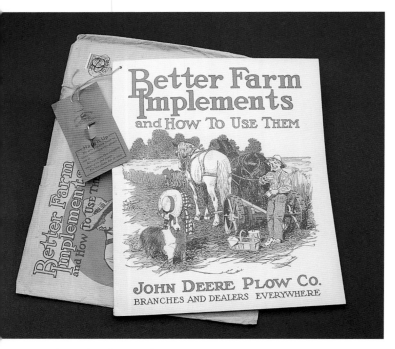

This 1915 edition of *Better Farm Implements and How to Use Them* is similar to the *Better Farming* and *Modern Farming* magazines. Issued by the John Deere Plow Company, this booklet still has its original mailing envelope and tag for hanging it up in the dealership. It includes product information on plows, hay rakes, binders, Van Brunt grain drills, disks, harrows, wagons, and such. *Nick Cedar*

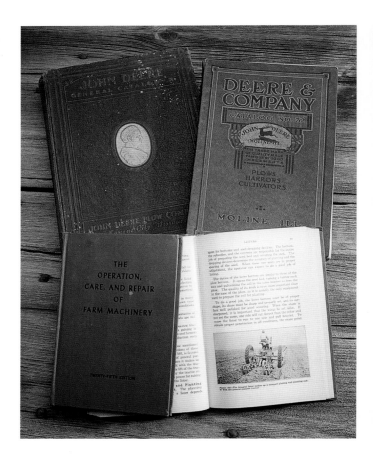

In the early 1900s, Deere issued General Catalogs that featured all the available equipment for that year. These two styles (upper left and right) are labeled "N" and "No. 32," making them from 1931 and 1912. The two smaller blue hardcover books titled *The Operation, Care, and Repair of Farm Machinery* provide educational information without being brand-specific. The 12th and 25th editions date back to 1938 and 1952, respectively. *Nick Cedar*

Deere & Company sent dealers large catalogs that included the full line of equipment available for the year. These books were often issued by each branch and showcased specific models for that region. The red hardcover book on the right is the *1924 John Deere General Catalog No. 1* from the Dallas, Texas, branch. In the middle, a blue leatherlike book from the Kansas City branch is labeled as *General Catalog – K*, which can be dated back to 1928. The smaller softbound book on the left is "No. 31" from 1911. Today, several of these 400-plus-page books can be added to a collection for about a dollar per page. *Denny Eilers*

As an equipment manufacturer for more than 160 years, John Deere has printed countless brochures detailing its products and services. These pieces of literature range from simple, economical fliers in black and white to colorful, multiple-page brochures.

Early literature was filled with sketches and illustrations. Photographs in black and white were added over the years, followed by full-color images of machinery at work in the field. Testimonials from satisfied customers graced the pages over the years, as did technical specifications and detailed measurements of the equipment featured. From basic essentials to comprehensive coverage, the range of John Deere literature from the past holds a fascinating place in company history. Today, even the racks that once held these brochures are highly collectible. Early wooden and metal versions with a complete set of literature can range in value from $100 to $1,000.

Of special interest to some collectors is the literature for unique or specialty products, such as very early editions of certain models, and equipment with a short life span or limited market coverage. Naturally, the early tractor pieces for the Waterloo Boy and the Model D tractors attract the attention of John Deere collectors. Some unique pieces of literature can add considerable value to a collection, such as brochures for specialty crop equipment, limited-production models, or anything released during the wartime effort.

Company letterheads and other corporate documents now serve as valued pieces of memorabilia. From personal letters and policy paperwork to sales receipts and repair tickets, documents related to John Deere allow collectors to capture bits and pieces of agricultural history. For interested collectors, much can be gleaned from these dusty documents and vintage stationery—names of company executives, prices for equipment, dates of important transactions, and so on. While some collectors prefer "clean" stationery (no writing), others find more value in "used" letterhead (with writing). Either way, these pieces of paper connect collectors with John Deere history.

Pretty pastoral scenes and bright birds accent this beautiful 1880s tri-fold brochure on the "Moline Broadcast Seeder" from Deere & Mansur. *Nick Cedar*

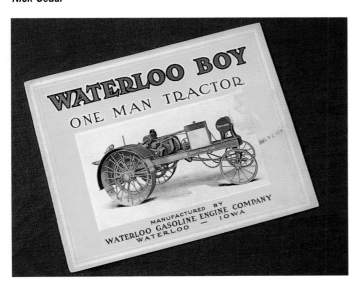

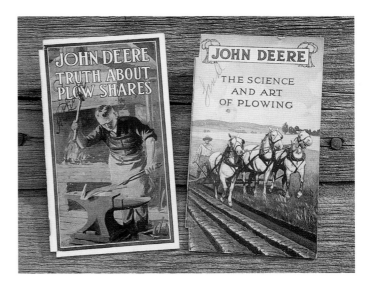

The plow is probably Deere's most famous product, which explains why the company printed several booklets on the topic. Hear the *Truth About Plow Shares* from the famed blacksmith and learn *The Science and Art of Plowing* from the inventor himself. These 30-page pieces date back to 1915 and 1919, respectively. The booklets tell farmers how to properly harness a team, how to work and rest the horses, and how draft plays a role in plowing. *Nick Cedar*

A 1914 Waterloo Boy brochure highlights the introduction of the Model R, which had a twin-cylinder, side-by-side engine that later became the famous "Poppin' Johnnie" style sold under the John Deere umbrella from 1918 to 1960. Note the chain steering and right-side radiator position. From 1914 to 1917, the Model R appeared in over a dozen different styles—A through M. *Brenda Kruse*

Froelich Builds the First Tractor

Engineering pioneer John Froelich built the first tractor in 1892, although the term "tractor" was not yet used. The Waterloo Gasoline Traction Engine Company of Waterloo, Iowa, touted this "gasoline traction engine" as the only one on earth. The inspiration for this innovative design came from farmers in the Dakotas who didn't have easy access to a wood or coal supply for steam-powered units.

Froelich mounted a Van Duzen stationary engine on a wood frame and the first tractor was born. Amazingly, this 16-horsepower machine was capable of moving both forward and backward. Unfortunately, Froelich's invention didn't instantly propel the Waterloo Gasoline Engine Company to fame and fortune. The stationary engine line kept the company afloat while Froelich experimented. By 1911, the company built the first official Waterloo Boy design, which later became part of John Deere's product line in 1918.

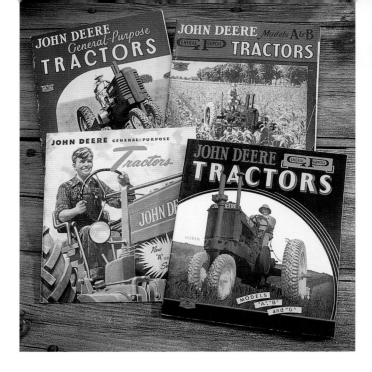

The Model A introduced in 1932 was billed as the "tractor for average farm work," and the smaller Model B tractor of 1933 was "for the lighter farm jobs." Henry Dreyfuss styled these popular General Purpose tractors in 1938, as shown on the upper left cover. The lower left cover is a 1947 version with electric start, lights, and armchair-type seat. The two brochures on the right show the unstyled models from 1937. The Model G featured in two of the brochures was introduced in 1937 as a more powerful alternative to the Model A. *Nick Cedar*

The Model D introduced in 1923 was the first full-production tractor designed by John Deere. The literature at the top may be in rough condition, but this 1930 edition is considered quite rare—and valued at $325 in mint condition. The colorful spread shown at the bottom is from a 1935 brochure. *Nick Cedar*

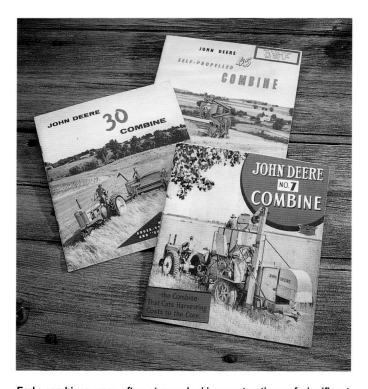

Early combines were often strange-looking contraptions of significant size. In fact, the No. 7 stood 13 feet high, stretched 23 feet behind the tractor, and weighed 5,420 pounds in transport. Models featured in these three product brochures include the pull-type No. 7 of 1939, the No. 45 self-propelled of 1956, and the pull-type No. 30 from 1958. *Nick Cedar*

These four pieces of literature show tractor designs from the early 1950s and 1960s. The Model MC track-type crawlers were a direct result of Deere's 1947 purchase of the Lindeman Manufacturing factory in Yakima, Washington. The tractor was made in Dubuque but used tracks from the renamed Yakima Works. The historic Model R diesel tractor introduced in 1948 was Deere's first diesel, and the first tractor with a live independent PTO and all-steel cab option. More than 21,000 units were built from 1948 to 1954. The Model 420 utility tractor came out in 1955 from the Dubuque Tractor Works factory. Designed to replace the 40 Series, the seven different models didn't look much different until June 1956, when the yellow panels were added to the finish. In 1963, Deere updated the 3010 and 4010 to become the Model 3020 and 4020 tractors. The 4020 later earned the most popular tractor honors of the 1960s, accounting for 48 percent of all 1966 sales. A new Power Shift transmission brought back the single-lever, forward-reverse operation first seen on the Dain All-Wheel Drive tractor of 1918. *Nick Cedar*

John Deere continues to produce educational information related to agriculture that is not specific to the equipment it sells. For example, these two booklets on *Hybrid Corn* from 1939 and *Soy Beans for Profit* from 1936 gave farmers additional guidance about plant spacing, hill drop, and lime and manure applications. The other booklet, entitled *What happens to old model John Deere tractors: As told by owners* was issued in 1954. Inside, it tells tales of how current customers use their older tractors for light-duty work, such as belt-pulley jobs. *Nick Cedar*

The onset of World War II greatly affected equipment manufacturers such as John Deere. By the mid-1940s, the government was enforcing material restrictions and production limitations to enhance the war effort. Deere's factories switched gears to build tank transmissions, ammunition, armored tractors, and even laundry units. More than 4,500 employees had entered military service by the end of the war, as had many of the farmers across the country. Even Charles Wiman was forced to leave his position as president of Deere & Company to serve as a colonel in the tank and combat vehicle division of the U.S. Army's Ordnance Corps. The end of the war brought significant changes to both employees and management at Deere & Company. This 1943 patriotic edition of *The Furrow* from Canada showcases Deere's war efforts, and the other booklet features advice on machinery repair in *How to Keep Your Farm Equipment in the Fight. Nick Cedar*

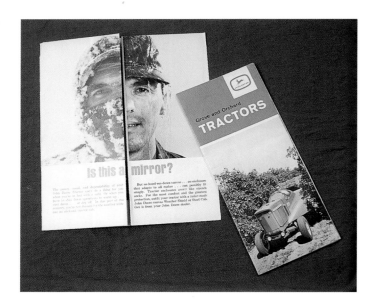

John Deere often produced smaller brochures highlighting its equipment for specialty markets. These two fold-out pieces promote John Deere tractor cabs (left) and Grove and Orchard tractors (right). The four-legged deer logo dates these brochures between 1956 and 1968. Judging from the tractor on the cover, this piece is from the 1960s, when Deere built the four-cylinder version of the New Generation models from in Waterloo. *Brenda Kruse*

Between 1971 and 1982, John Deere manufactured nearly 225,000 snowmobiles at its Horicon, Wisconsin, factory. This product brochure highlights the "Big John" and "Little John" models available, as well as a full line of clothing and accessories for winter fun. *Brenda Kruse*

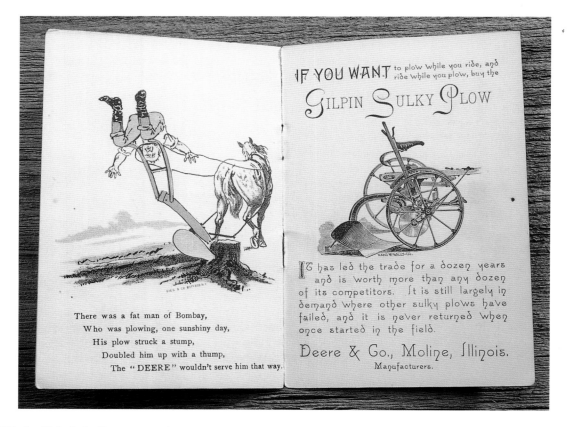

Introduced in 1875, the Gilpin Sulky Plow was a riding unit rather than a walk-behind one. While not the first successful sulky plow, it became one of the most popular in the country by 1880, to the point that the Moline factory could hardly keep up with orders. Designed by Gilpin Moore, owner of 35 patents for engineering excellence, the Gilpin Sulky Plow led the industry for 12 years according to this humorous "Book of Verses" from 1887. The illustration clearly shows one of the advantages of the riding plow: "There was a fat man of Bombay, Who was plowing, one sunshiny day, His plow struck a stump, Doubled him up with a thump, The 'DEERE' wouldn't serve him that way." *Nick Cedar*

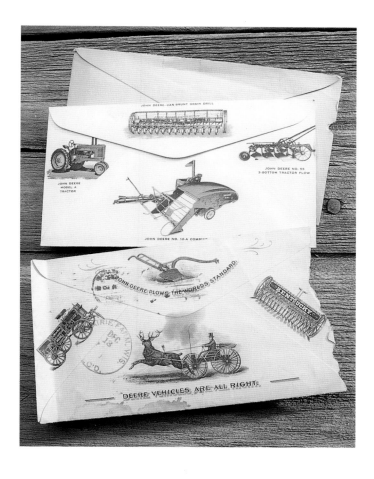

Envelopes of the past were often more colorful and artistic than today's boring, businesslike designs. These three pieces display brightly colored lithographs of equipment and logos on both the front and back. One is from the Wagon Works in 1927; another is an unused envelope from Romer Mercantile & Grain Co., Dove Creek, Colorado; and the bottom envelope is postmarked 1910 from Deere & Webber in Minneapolis. On the reverse, this last one shows artwork of a plow, "Moline" wagon, Kentucky drill, and a deer pulling a buggy with the phrase "Deere Vehicles Are All Right" all in blue ink. The middle envelope (ca. 1940) uses green-and-yellow art to depict a styled Model A tractor, John Deere-Van Brunt grain drill, No. 55 three-bottom tractor plow, and the No. 12A combine. *Nick Cedar*

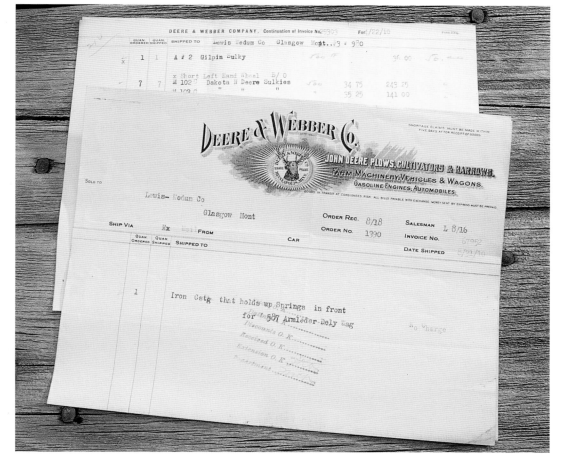

Invoices were issued for every piece of John Deere equipment ever sold. These documents can add interesting details to company history. This sale bill dated August 31, 1910, shows that a Gilpin sulky and seven Dakota sulkies were shipped to a Glasgow, Montana, dealership at a price of about $35 per machine. The letterhead imprint is from the Minneapolis branch, the Deere & Webber Company. Note the products listed: "John Deere Plows, Cultivators & Harrows. Farm Machinery, Vehicles & Wagons. Gasoline Engines, Automobiles." *Nick Cedar*

These little notebooks and booklets advertise buggies, corn planters, and the Omaha branch. The white notebook (top) shows the Omaha warehouse in 1903. The blue booklet (right) of 1880–1881 promotes the Deere Rotary Drop Corn Planter made by Deere & Mansur Company. Inside pages have notebook lines and an ad for the Moline Spring Stalk Cutter. The white booklet (left) advertises John Deere plows and White Elephant Vehicles from the St. Louis branch, which started selling "white" (unfinished) buggies as early as 1883. By 1891, the Mansur & Tebbetts Carriage Manufacturing Company built a factory. John Deere purchased the Mansur & Tebbetts businesses in 1899, and the Mansur & Tebbetts Implement Company name changed to the John Deere Plow Company of St. Louis in 1901. It was later incorporated as the Reliance Buggy Company in 1913. *Nick Cedar*

This trio of wooden print blocks once promoted "Deere Corn Planters: The Most Accurate Drop," a Deere & Mansur Company logo, and a factory scene from Deere & Mansur in Moline. *Nick Cedar*

This assortment of copper-type print blocks shows the intricate detail of artwork and trademarks from Deere & Company over the years. The 1936 shield logo and 1950 Quality Farm Equipment logo are shown here. The stag deer artwork matches the middle of the Deere & Mansur trademark. Two of the blocks promote corn planters from Deere & Mansur. One shows a General Purpose tractor with a logo similar to the one used from 1912 to 1936. *Nick Cedar*

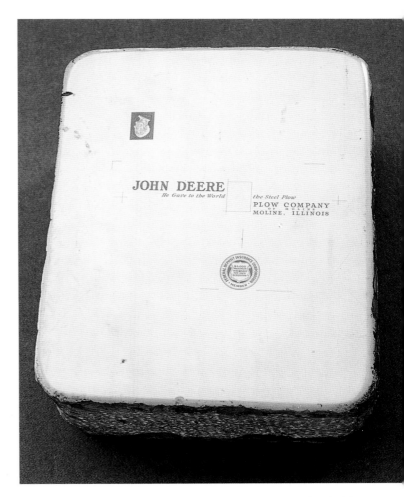

Used in printing processes, this large lithograph stone is imprinted with a stationery design. Note the bust of John Deere and Federal Deposit Insurance Corporation (FDIC) seal with the words "He gave the world the steel plow" from "John Deere Plow Company of Moline." This 10-pound block measures 6.25 inches high, 5.25 inches wide, and 3 inches thick. The FDIC first insured banking deposits in 1934, making this piece some time after that. *Nick Cedar*

These two wooden print blocks show artwork of two tractors designed by Deere & Company. The top block depicts a large-bore General Purpose tractor (1930–1935) with the three-legged, leaping-over-the-log trademark (1912–1936). The bottom print block has a styled Model A tractor with electric lights (1947–1952) and cultivator plus a Quality Farm Equipment logo (1950–1956). *Nick Cedar*

Calendars give companies a daily reminder and a yearlong promotional presence in the home or office of the customer. That's why John Deere has been issuing an annual printed calendar since 1890. From the traditional wall-hung version to the smaller *Farmer's Pocket Companion*, calendars from John Deere continue to be a part of the company's promotional efforts. This annual rite of passage is often met with a fair share of anticipation among John Deere enthusiasts. A 1999 edition even focused on collectibles, including many of the items also featured in this book.

As early as 1866, John Deere printed an annual *Farmer's Pocket Companion* for dealers to give to customers. These 6.5x3.5-inch booklets served as a calendar and diary or notebook. Along with helpful charts for measurements and the like, ads with elaborate artwork promoting John Deere products graced the pages. Covers were sometimes quite colorful; others were drab for the sake of economy.

After 1910, these items were commonly called *Pocket Ledgers*, which John Deere still prints today, although it does not seem to be as popular a giveaway with dealers.

Starting in the 1930s, Deere also produced a larger ledger called *The Handy Farm Account Book*, which gave customers more room for recordkeeping. These annual booklets helped farmers take inventory, value assets, and track receipts, expenses, repairs, and depreciation.

Finding a ledger or calendar in good shape is the key to adding value to a collection. For maximum value, covers should not be soiled or damaged, all pages must be intact, and it would preferably have very little (if any) writing inside. However, some collectors are quite interested in the historical information transcribed inside these booklets. One collector who bought several ledgers over a few months sat down to study them one winter evening and actually discovered that one had been in his own family!

Also called "pocket ledgers," these miniature journals gave farmers a convenient place to track expenses, income, and other farm-related information. These three diaries date back to 1878, 1903, and 1905. *Nick Cedar*

The "pocket companion" pieces shown here date back to 1883, 1886, 1890, 1899, and 1903. Editions from the late 1800s and early 1900s might bring $150–$300 apiece. *Nick Cedar*

From the Freeman Brothers of Gouverneur, New York, this simple 1945 calendar shows the "V for Victory" color artwork with the woman working in the field while the military trucks pass by on the road. During World War II, "Rosie the Riveter" came to represent the women on the home front who kept America working. *Michelle Schueder*

This large centennial calendar from 1937 still has its original cover sheet and parchment paper with a unique weblike pattern. The special medallion has the bust of John Deere on one side (shown) and the centennial design on the reverse (visible on the lower right corner of the calendar). Measuring 20x27 inches, this prized possession in mint condition with its box could be worth up to $700. *Nick Cedar*

Colorful. Attention-getting. Entertaining. These three adjectives describe the printed promotional material from John Deere. Whether it's pocket-sized trade cards or wall-sized posters, John Deere promotional paper is highly collectible today. Most collectors also consider advertisements and annual reports as worthy memorabilia.

Postcards and trade cards are often the most colorful examples of any John Deere printed piece. Early editions rarely focused on the equipment's features and benefits. Often, non-farm scenes decorated these artful cards instead. Salesmen would either mail or hand out these cards to prospects. Later editions showed equipment in action with actual photographs instead of fancy artwork. Several postcards of factory scenes were printed and given out to whoever toured the plant.

Available in numerous sizes, posters pulled double duty as promotional tools for dealers and educational vehicles for salesmen. Most were hung in dealerships, but some were given to customers for decorating their shop walls.

Large, detailed posters also served as teaching aids to help a salesperson educate a customer on how a piece of equipment worked.

Advertisements were published in local newspapers and regional trade magazines in hopes of catching the attention and interest of farmers in the market for John Deere equipment. Again, these range from basic black-and-white illustrations to full-color photography. While today's corporate budgets for advertising and promotion make finding copies of recent ads easier, many earlier versions are considered very scarce and quite valuable as a result.

Annual reports for shareholders of Deere & Company were first issued in 1912. In addition to financial statements, these documents also included a review of the year's activities. Only the very earliest of editions hold much value as a collectible, but recent reports can also provide plenty of educational information that may be of interest to a collector.

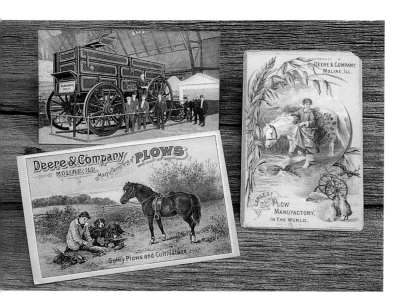

Above: Trade cards from John Deere often featured colorful scenes that had little to do with farming. Here, a pheasant hunting scene and a woman with a horse at the water's edge promote John Deere's "sulky plows and cultivators" and the "Largest Plow Manufactory in the World." The postcard (upper left) advertises the "giant 'Moline' wagon, the biggest wagon in the world." Built double the scale of the New Moline wagon, this mammoth measured 42 feet long, 12 feet wide, and 16 feet high. Its box held 640 bushels of small grains or 350 bushels of corn. Made for promotional purposes only, the big wagon cost $1,903.48 to build in 1907. *Nick Cedar*

Right: After building a grain binder and a corn binder for 15 years, Deere's Harvester Works designed the corn picker and the combine around 1925. That year, 23 prototypes helped with the corn harvest in the Midwest. The No. 127 one-row corn picker was the star of this 1954 poster. *Denny Eilers*

Right: A colorful 1920 poster explained the accuracy advantages of the No. 999 planter from John Deere. This wire check-row model became world-famous and remained in the line until after World War II. *Denny Eilers*

Below: This 1954 poster promoted the "70" Standard tractor capable of pulling a four- to five-bottom plow. Introduced in March 1953, the Model 70 Series replaced the Model G. The "standard" model had an adjustable front axle that gave five tread widths from 52 to 68 inches. *Denny Eilers*

Left: This creative piece of artwork shows a team of bullfrogs hitched to a Moline Wagon with a frog family inside. The somewhat rhyming verse at the bottom says: "A frog he would a riding go, O Ho! O Ho! His girl and boy and wife also (just as above is seen) and on the road they were not slow for they quickly distanced friend and foe says the owl to his mate in the tree Ho, Ho! It's that wagon from Moline." This artwork (reprinted in 1990) was originally applied to a dustpan back in the late 1890s and is now on display in the Girard Mural of ag-related antiques at Deere & Company headquarters. *Denny Eilers*

Below: This little folding card says: "Farmer, open this gate and you will see something Deere to your heart." On the inside, it shows a colorful scene of a man plowing, with the words, "Our Trade Mark is the Leaping Deer," and a place for "Our Agent" to stamp his name. The logo at the top is quite unique in that it doesn't match any official trademark designs. One can only guess that this 4.5x2.5-inch piece is possibly as old as the 1880s. Depending on condition, this "Farmer Gate" fold-out could be worth $150–$300. *Nick Cedar*

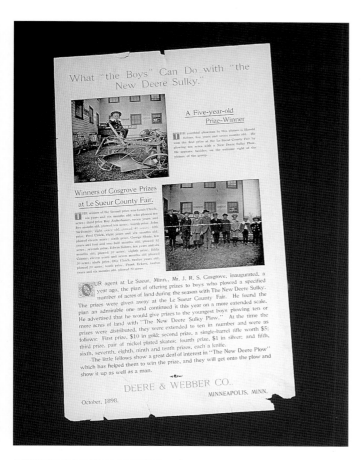

This advertisement from October 1898 tells the story of a plowing contest at the LeSueur County Fair, organized by Agent J.R. Cosgrove of Deere & Webber in Minneapolis. The headline reads "What 'the Boys' Can Do with 'the New Deere Sulky.'" A four-year-old who plowed 10 acres took top honors and is pictured on the plow along with a group photo of all 10 winners. The following prizes were awarded: "First prize, $10 in gold; Second prize, a single-barrel rifle worth $5; Third prize, pair of nickel plated skates; Fourth prize, $1 in silver; and fifth, sixth, seventh, eighth, ninth and tenth prizes, each a knife." *Denny Eilers*

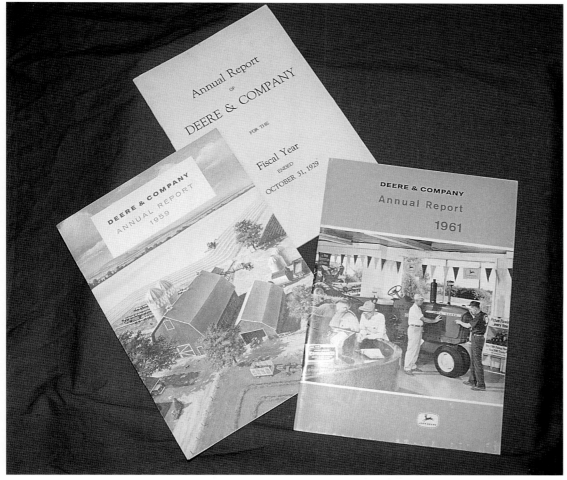

Annual reports summarize Deere's activities for shareholders and other interested parties. Today, the older editions of these reports are collectible. In addition, these pieces serve as excellent resources for information to help date other memorabilia or events. Older versions were plain and simple booklets similar to the 1929 annual report at the top. The other two (1956 and 1961) have colorful covers. Recent annual reports use classy, understated designs with lots of black and gold. *Brenda Kruse*

CHAPTER 5

Antique Iron:
Parts and Pieces of the Past

For folks who "bleed green," collecting anything and everything associated with John Deere includes parts and pieces from tractors and other equipment. Some people specialize in collecting the granddaddy of all collectibles—antique iron. However, collecting parts and pieces may be the next best thing for those who don't have the space to store dozens of full-size tractors, or the skill to restore rusty relics back to their original showroom shine. From serial number plates and seats to gauges and grilles, anything that was once a part of John Deere equipment is fair game for an interested collector. Of obvious interest are castings branded with the John Deere name or logo.

Other than the actual parts and pieces of equipment, tools and toolboxes are also very popular collectibles. Wrenches, in particular, have a strong following, as witnessed by an extensive book on this sole topic. Written by P. T. Rathbone, *The History of Old-Time Farm Implement Companies & the Wrenches They Issued* (1999) provides thorough coverage of the category.

Not to be left out, cans, cartons, and other packaging also count as collectibles in this category. Whether it's an old parts sack or a carton of spark plugs, some collectors appreciate the challenge of locating items that most people would throw away.

Above: The word "Deere" stamped on anything makes it collectible. These wrenches are identified by parts numbers, which associate the tool with a particular piece of equipment and period of time. *Nick Cedar*

Left: From rusty wrenches and cast-iron seats, collecting parts and pieces of equipment is just one aspect of the market for John Deere memorabilia. Items shown include a "Power" fold-out poster in Model D tractor literature, toolbox lid with 1937 trademark logo, green oil can with spout (Part No. JD 93), Velie Motors Corporation hubcap, 1996 pewter Christmas ornament, belt buckle with epoxy swirl inset and tractor, Deere Mansur Co. wrench (A523), iridescent centennial marble with base, two-cylinder tractor matchbook, plastic tape measure with Moline dealer imprint, Velie Wrought-Iron Vehicles needlecase, Van Brunt Manufacturing employee badge, and a bullet pencil on keychain with Iowa dealer imprint. *Nick Cedar*

As a manufacturer of tractors and implements, John Deere also provided customers with specific tools to make appropriate adjustments and perform certain servicing procedures. These multipurpose tools often accompanied a new piece of equipment as it was sold from the dealership.

Tractor and implement wrenches are commonly collected today, as are the toolboxes that once held them. Some of the toolboxes bolted onto the tongues of implements, while others mounted directly on the frame.

A part number is typically cast into the tool, which helps collectors identify their finds. Engineering advancements, however, often led to the transformation of these tools. In fact, there are several instances of wrenches that look different but have the same part number! In some cases, the original tool was modified to perform another function, but a new part number was not issued.

While it can be time-consuming, the best way to identify a particular part number is to study parts books or illustrations of equipment in catalogs and brochures. Usually, the tool's corresponding part number is listed, allowing a collector to associate it with a particular piece of equipment, its purpose, its age, and its original price.

This grouping of John Deere wrenches includes tools for buggies, binders, cultivators, and manure spreaders. Each cast-iron wrench is stamped with the word "Deere" and a part number. The "A196A" wrenches were used on 1912-style walking cultivators as listed in a 1934 Plow Works catalog. Note how the lettering differs between the three almost-identical wrenches. The "HZ836" wrench was used on grain and corn binders as stated in a 1920 John Deere Harvester Works catalog. The large "Deere & Co." wrench accompanied plows and Deere "World" cultivators as listed in a 1907 Plow Works catalog and the 1916 Deere Catalog "K." The "7321-C" looks a little like a bottle opener, but this wrench patented in 1903 probably came with horse-drawn buggies. According to a 1914 Marseilles Works catalog, the "John Deere" wrench was used on manure spreaders. *Nick Cedar*

The inscriptions on these four wrenches connect these tools to the Deere & Mansur Company. The large wrench (B470) at the top was listed in a 1915 parts book for use on disc cultivators from 1900 to 1907 and on disc harrows from 1905 to 1908. The uniquely shaped tool in the middle is more of a mystery. Collectors suspect this was used on planters in the early 1880s. The two smaller, simpler wrenches (A522 and A523) were used on new Deere cylinder loaders starting in 1900. *Nick Cedar*

This assortment of wrenches belongs to Dain hay equipment, which was first manufactured in Missouri around 1881. The two wrenches at the top (#J81) are similar designs and were used on hay stackers. The wrench marked "Dain Mfg. Co." on the front and "Ottumwa, Ia." on the reverse, was shown in a 1901 Deere & Mansur catalog, dating it shortly after Dain moved the factory to Ottumwa. The wrench below shows the other variation with "Carrollton, Mo." on one side. It likely dates between 1890 and 1900, when the factory was located there. Notice the slight differences in lettering and edging. The clawlike "Z78" tool was used on Dain mowers as verified in a 1920 Harvester Works catalog. The wrench on the lower left is for a hay loader found in a 1901 Deere & Mansur catalog. *Nick Cedar*

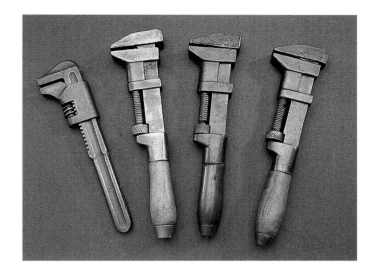

The Syracuse Chilled Plow Company of Syracuse, New York, built plows for East Coast farmers starting in 1879 (see large wrench with "SCP Co." engraving). John Deere purchased the company in 1911. The identical "Z2" wrenches can be found with either "Syracuse" or "John Deere" on the handle. These were used on a two-way sulky plow, as shown in the Deere Catalog "K" of 1916. In all likelihood, the "Z2" wrenches were also used on earlier equipment. The two other wrenches shown here are inscribed with "Wood Beam" and "Iron & Steel" to denote the type of plow. *Nick Cedar*

This quartet of monkey wrenches represents the two styles—wooden-handle (three on the right) and all-steel (far left). The wrench (#HZ6758) on the left with "Deere" inscribed in its head was used on binders and mowers according to a 1920 Harvester Works catalog. The three 10-inch wrenches with wooden handles (#HZ5322) were also used on binders and mowers. One says "John Deere," another reads "Deere Harvester," and the far right one is inscribed "Deere & Co." on its head. *Nick Cedar*

These two wrenches belong to the Van Brunt line of grain drills. The top tool is the original wrench from 1911, while the bottom one commemorates the 75th anniversary in 1986. *Nick Cedar*

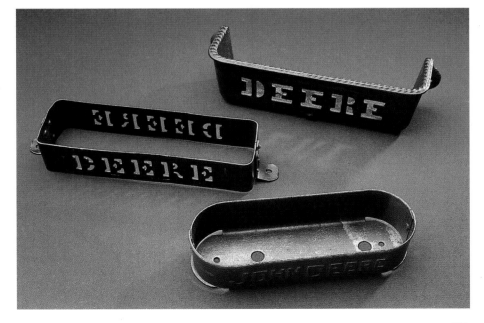

Toolbox designs were as diverse as the Deere equipment on which they were mounted. The "John Deere" one (lower right) and the bottomless cut-out "Deere" toolbox (middle left) bolted to the top of an implement's tongue. The heavy cast-iron three-sided toolbox (upper right) attached to the side of a beam on horse-drawn riding plows and cultivators. *Nick Cedar*

To today's collector, just about any part or piece from John Deere equipment is fair game. For tractors, that includes everything from radiators and mufflers to hubcaps and hourmeters, even steering wheels and the actual wheels! For implements, the list ranges from planter lids and boxes to plow footrests, levers, and the like. While many of the parts and pieces from implements are widely available today, most of the parts for two-cylinder tractors have been squirreled away by ambitious restorers.

When it comes to John Deere equipment, some of the strangest parts and pieces were given official part numbers.

A hand, a foot pedal, and a step are a few of the more unusual finds. In general, any casting branded with the John Deere name is likely to draw a crowd of collectors at an auction.

No matter what the part or piece, it takes a little research to locate and identify its origin based on its part number. By flipping through the pages of parts catalogs, a persistent person can usually solve the mystery. Yet in some cases, the lack of a part number or even the absence of a listing can frustrate collectors in their quest to officially identify an item.

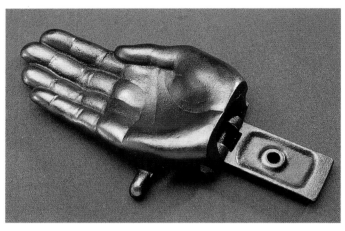

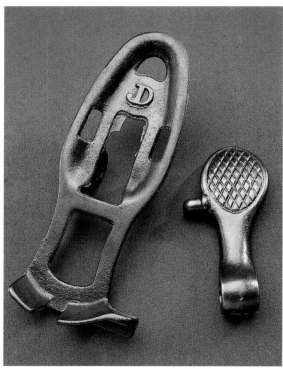

Perhaps the most unique item ever found in a John Deere parts catalog is #Y1656. Illustrated in a 1907 repair book, this cast-iron hand once hinged to a display model that demonstrated the accurate kernel-dropping ability of a Deere & Mansur corn planter. As the story goes, the horse-drawn planter was mounted onto a stand equipped with a motor. A mechanical device then dropped corn into this casting of a hand so the customer could see how many kernels dropped each time. The hand tripped at every dropping, giving customers a lesson on the precision of a Deere & Mansur planter. *Nick Cedar*

The large foot pedal on the left (part #B114H) belonged to a "Light-Running New John Deere Binder" starting in 1923. It was also used on a straight-drop bundle carrier. The tiny pedal on the right (part #Y806) was used as a scraper roller pedal on No. 35 and No. 36 corn and cotton planters as early as 1912. *Nick Cedar*

While this may look more like a gladiator weapon from ancient Rome, this piece of equipment is actually an early version of the row marker. Attached by a chain to the rear of a narrow track sower, this 9-inch-long shaft trails in the dirt, leaving behind a marked line to follow on the next round. Part number "H39M" listed for 45 cents in a 1916 parts catalog. *Nick Cedar*

Planters weren't the only piece of John Deere equipment to feature cast-iron lids. These items are also popular because they, too, feature the John Deere name and trademark symbol. The two on the left are toolbox lids from mowers made in the 1920s and 1930s. The round one (lower right) has its part number right on top (#4586-C), identifying it as part of a No. 2 1/2 spring corn sheller from 1919 to 1924. The large lid (upper right) from the "Dain Mf'g Co. Ottumwa Ia." goes on a Vertical Lift mower made between 1912 and 1914. *Nick Cedar*

In 1899, Deere & Company officially entered the buggy business by buying the Mansur & Tebbetts Carriage Company of St. Louis. By 1913, the vehicle manufacturing business became the Reliance Buggy Company. However, the horse-drawn vehicle line only lasted until 1923, when Deere began building tractors. This cast-iron step with brass "Deere" inset cannot be positively identified, but appears to be similar to one shown on a four-passenger surrey. Typically, the step was only provided for rear-seat passengers—those riding in the front seat used the wheel hub as a step. *Nick Cedar*

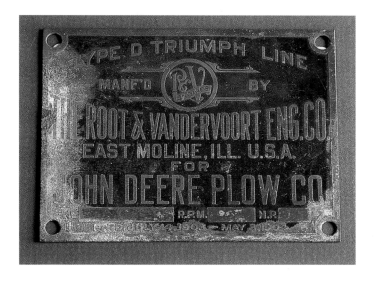

This corroded serial tag serves as a rusty reminder of the Type D Triumph engine manufactured for the John Deere Plow Company by the Root and Vandervoort Engine Company of East Moline. Patent dates listed are July 14, 1903, and May 3, 1904. The engine tag also has areas for the serial number, rpm, and horsepower. *Denny Eilers*

"Gilpin" is another name that some might not quickly associate with John Deere. The name stands for Deere engineer Gilpin Moore, who designed the "Gilpin" sulky plow in 1875. The patented design won a plowing contest at the Paris Exhibition of 1878. By 1900, it was a best-selling unit and was produced until after World War II. In 1881, a "power-lift" device was added to the plow so it could be easily raised out of the ground. The cast-iron toolbox (upper right) and footrest (lower left) were also part of the machine at this time. *Nick Cedar*

These contraptions were actually early hand-planting devices called the "Paragon" and the "Buckeye." These two styles of hand corn planters were listed in an 1898–1899 catalog from the Kansas City and Denver branches. A simple design of wooden handles paired with a seed box of sheet iron let farmers fill in missing plants within the row. The "Paragon" (left) sold for $10 per dozen; the advanced rotary drop action of the "Buckeye" (right) sold for $14 a dozen. *Nick Cedar/Denny Eilers*

For the most part, early pressed-steel planter lids were quite simple in design. On the left lid, it seems that the space in the middle was intended for the leaping deer, yet the logo is not there. Note the early-style, four-legged log-leaping deer stamped into the lid on the right. These 8-inch-diameter tin lids belonged on corn planters marketed by John Deere in the 1910s. *Nick Cedar*

Cast-iron planter lids usually included a ring as well as the hinged lid. Measuring about 7 inches in diameter, these Deere & Mansur Company lids were part of the No. 9 corn planter made from 1901 to 1907, as listed in a 1915 parts catalog. The underside states the following: "Patented Nov. 28, 1893. Reissued July 23, 1895. Patented Sept. 10, 1901, Y1521." Today, lids like these can bring up to $80 each as collectibles. *Nick Cedar*

This large (10 inches tall) cast-iron piece is actually an end of the grain box from a "Moline Broadcast Seeder." Note the standing deer symbol, which is similar to the ones on planter lids. Identified as part number L-1, this was first used in 1885. A larger size (L-35) was also used between 1886 and 1908. *Nick Cedar*

A little paint goes a long way in dressing up this cast-iron planter lid, as shown here on its box from an early Deere & Mansur corn planter. While the original version wasn't painted as beautifully as this, the artistic talents of a gifted person make this a prized possession in any collection. *Nick Cedar*

These two cast-iron lids depict the very different designs that are available as collectibles today. The lid on the left is 7 inches in diameter, while the one on the right measures 8 inches across. The smaller lid on the left shows a logo used in the early 1900s. The cast-iron lid with red paint for Deere & Mansur is nicknamed the "big-nosed deer" or "bull-nosed" design because of the prominent snout of the deer compared to other versions. Compared to the other stag scene with mountains in the background, this simpler design has raised edges to the lettering and artwork. According to a 1915 parts book, this lid ("Y3025") was used on the "No. 99 New Deere Corn Planter" introduced in 1911. *Nick Cedar*

This colorful tri-fold brochure promotes the "Mansur Check-Row Corn Planter" made by Deere & Mansur in the 1880s. The rotary-drop design of the metering device allowed seed to be placed in the ground one at a time. This worked well with an attachment called the "check-rower," which used knotted wires or rope to trip the rotary drop. Note the spool of wire positioned under the seat. The result was a checkerboardlike pattern that allowed for cross-cultivation. This popular planting method was used well into the 1930s. *Nick Cedar*

This wooden planter box can be found on the Rotary Drop Corn Planter made in the late 1870s by the Deere & Mansur Company. Measuring approximately 9.5x13x7 inches, this crude box was paired with another one on the original planter. In between the two boxes was a "dropper seat" where someone sat to operate the dropper lever when the planter's forward movement crossed a certain mark. *Nick Cedar*

Collectors consider cast-iron seats one of the premier parts and pieces available. Although rather large, awkward, and quite heavy, these uncomfortable seats have (thankfully) disappeared from implement and tractor designs of today. One look at these unforgiving seats makes it easy to understand why many farmers chose to stand up for their daily duties rather than flatten their rumps with every bump. Tractor operators welcomed the day in 1947 when the Model A's steel rounded-rump seat was replaced with a cushioned armchair-type seat. Tractor seats of today are plush marvels of comfort complete with lumbar support, adjustable armrests, air-ride, and even electric heaters to keep rear-ends toasty warm on a bone-chilling winter day!

Stamped-steel versions later replaced the cast-iron seats. Somewhat shaped in the form of an average farmer's rear, most seats have cut-out designs to provide a little "air conditioning" to the derriere. Today, the number of holes or slots is one way to identify the design, such as the nine-hole or the thirty-six-slot. Depending on the type and condition, cast-iron seats range in value from $200 to $500; stamped-steel versions can be found for $50 to $150 each.

This cast-iron "Deere & Co., Moline, Ill." seat could be found on riding plows like the Gilpin Sulky from the 1880s to the early 1900s. When horse-drawn implements moved from walk-behind designs to riding or sulky machines, cast-iron seats served as a leg-saving perch for farmers. *Nick Cedar*

This ornate round seat came from a Deere & Mansur corn planter. It is believed that the "dropper" or "check-rower" person sat on this 11.5-inch-diameter seat when planting was a two-man operation back in the late 1800s and early 1900s. *Nick Cedar*

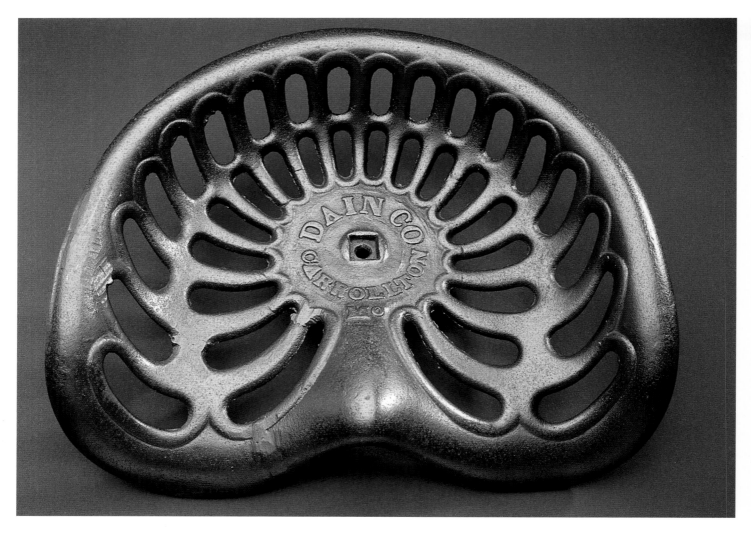

This well-rounded seat with plenty of cut-out "air coolers" most likely came from haying equipment made in the late 1800s by Dain Manufacturing of Carrollton, Missouri. In 1900, Dain moved his plant to Ottumwa, Iowa, where it became a John Deere property in 1911. *Nick Cedar*

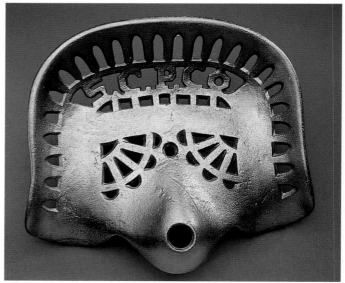

Some collectors might overlook this seat, thinking the "S.C.P. Co." meant nothing to John Deere. Before Deere bought the factory in 1911, the Syracuse Chilled Plow Company of Syracuse, New York, made plows as early as 1879. This crudely ornate seat probably fit a sulky plow. *Nick Cedar*

Whether it's a cloth bag, paper sack, cardboard box, or metal can, any container that once held something "John Deere green" piques the interest of a diehard collector. Many major brand names produced parts for John Deere. Cartons listing Delco Remy, Champion, or Fairbanks Morse garner added attention and value.

Oil cans may be the most interesting item, although tiny cardboard parts boxes smudged with greasy fingerprints

may also attract multiple bids at an auction. Today, the sacks that dealers sent home with customers are almost as collectible as the parts themselves. Considering that these cloth or paper bags were probably tossed soon after reaching the customer's machine shed, these unusual items can be challenging to find. Containers and packages that survive the seasons are often water-spotted, greasy, ripped, and sunfaded. Naturally, the condition affects the value accordingly.

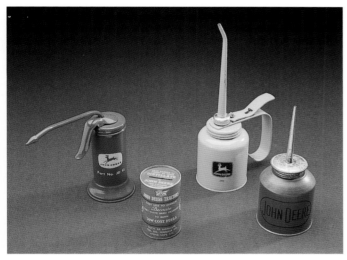

Oil cans of assorted varieties add to the collectible category. The red can (JD60H, far right) also exists in blue, green, and yellow colors with black lettering. Most say "John Deere," but some have a dealer name instead. The tall yellow oil can with pump (JD92) is a recent design from after 1968, judging by its logo. The small green can with yellow lettering is actually a coin bank made in 1937 for Deere's centennial. It promotes the "low cost fuels" used by John Deere two-cylinder tractors. The green oil can with pump (far left) shows the four-legged logo from 1956 with an identifying part number (JD93). *Nick Cedar*

This case of spark plugs (#AH830-R) was "manufactured expressly for John Deere Tractor Company by Champion Spark Plug Co., Toledo, Ohio." Note the Quality Farm Equipment logo, dating this item between 1950 and 1955. *Nick Cedar*

This grouping of oil cans and parts boxes ranges in condition from near-new to well-worn. A green oil can with dealer imprint (JD60H) can also be found in other colors. The two tiny oil cans are probably fake, say some collectors, due to their sticker-type decals. The large gold and black can is now doing duty as a coin bank. The small parts boxes bear logos from 1950 and 1956. *Michelle Schueder*

John Deere's Fertilizer Venture

One of the more mysterious aspects of the Deere story involves the brief history of the John Deere Chemical Company in Pryor, Oklahoma, from 1952 to 1965. According to company historians, Charles Wiman instigated the venture after a visit to the U.S. Department of Agriculture in Washington. That's when Wiman was convinced that fertilizer manufacturing was a viable proposition for Deere & Company. He then proposed the idea to the board and fought until it was approved.

The authors of a *Forbes* magazine article on the story wrote highly of Wiman's scheme:

Deere's soundskulled [sic] country boys can see a mite beyond the visible horizon. A foothold in synthetic fertilizers will work double dividends, they calculate. In the 13-state midwestern corn and wheat belt which Deere figures to supply from Pryor, nitro-fertilizer demand in 1955 is expected to quadruple 1950's consumption. Corn planters are learning that nitrates increase per-acre yield from 40 to 100 bushels. By thus aiding the farmer (tentative plans call for selling bulk urea, non-trademarked, to fertilizer makers) to more abundant harvests, demand for machinery will become more abundant too.

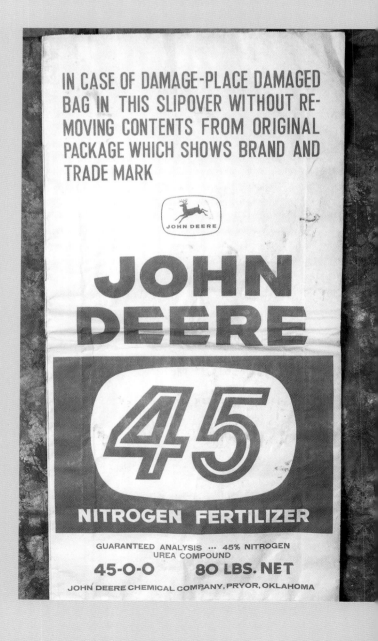

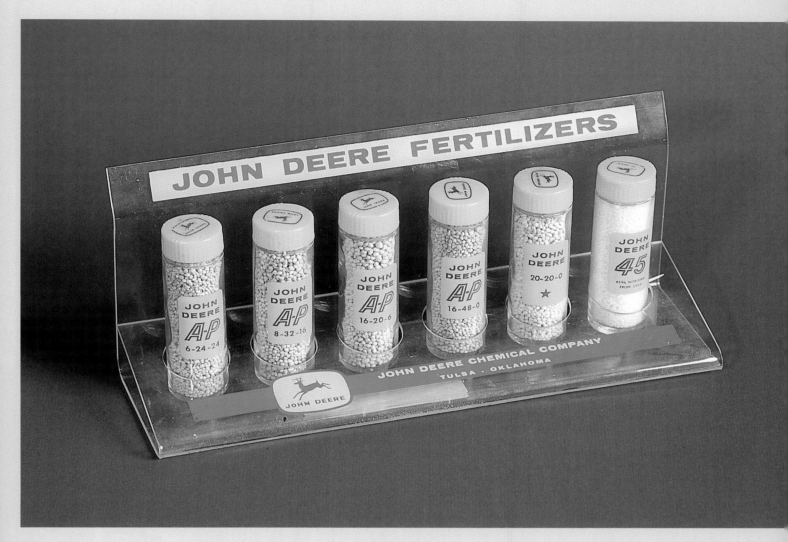

These items represent Deere's involvement in the fertilizer industry: (far left) a soil sample bag, (left) a bulk fertilizer bag, and a dealer counter display (above) showing the available concentrations. *Nick Cedar/Michelle Schueder/Denny Eilers*

Scale-model replicas of the famous green-and-yellow equipment give farm toy collectors a miniature version of the full-size machine. An assortment of John Deere toy tractors and implements adds to the variety of memorabilia on the collectible market. Items shown include a 1/16 scale toy disk harrow with box from Eska-Carter, "Soil Fertilizers" educational booklet, gold 150th anniversary display plate, John Deere Day 1994 belt buckle, gang plow educational lantern slide, Dain hay equipment trade cards, John Deere Forms 1998 pin with tracked Model 8000 tractor, gold dice-shaped cube with 1968-1999 trademark, brushed aluminum keychain with 1956 trademark, pewter snowmobile charm bracelet, gold "John Deere Company, Kansas City, Mo." token, pewter "John Deere Quality Parts" clutch pin, and a leather Titewad wallet with bust of John Deere. *Nick Cedar*

CHAPTER 6

Toys: Honey, I Shrunk the John Deere

These days, farm toys aren't just for kids. Scale-model replicas of real tractors and matching implements also appeal to those who are young at heart. Granted, most collectible toys rarely spend a day in the dirt, because values are significantly higher for "New in the Box" toys. Yet no one can deny that toy collecting is a fun-filled hobby—even a profitable business to a few lucky ones who are able to pair their passion with a paycheck.

From the earliest Vindex scale models to the latest Mary's Moo Moos™ figurines and Danbury Mint® releases, toy collecting has certainly seen significant success in the past . . . and the trend doesn't appear to be slowing. Today's toy shows and museums attract large crowds of fans young and old who come to admire the miniature models.

Over the years, toys have developed their own cultlike following, as one can see by the number of magazines, books, and other resources dedicated to toy collectors. One such resource is the *Toy Farmer* magazine. Several knowledgeable individuals have written a wide variety of books and guides specifically on John Deere toys. For those interested in values, *Dick's Farm Toy Price Guide & Check List* has emerged as a reliable source. For a full list of related resources, see the appendix at the back of the book.

Toy collecting can be divided into three major categories: tractors, implements, and pedal tractors. More

often than not, toy collectors are also drawn to life-size versions of John Deere tractors. Yet, compared to collecting farm toys, restoring antique tractors is certainly a more challenging hobby, as it requires more space, skill, and money. Miniature models make it easier to amass a large collection, especially when it comes to displaying the items—no need to own several machine sheds!

The closest thing to full-size equipment is a patent model or salesman's sample. Although technically not true toys, they are still miniature models of farm equipment, making these demonstration units collectible as well. Often highly intricate to illustrate all working parts, these detailed designs in 1/6 or 1/8 scale let the salesman show customers how the machinery worked. Because few are known to exist, these "special" samples are hard to find and, therefore, extremely valuable.

Today, die-cast steel is by far the favorite method for manufacturing modern farm toys. But over the years, the type of material used in scale-model production evolved from wood, tin, and crude cast iron to pressed steel, sand-cast aluminum, pewter, even rubber and plastic.

Not all John Deere toys are manufactured in the United States. Some of the later Ertl models have been contracted out to Korea, China, or Singapore for production. Other scale-model manufacturers build John Deere toys in Canada, Germany, Argentina, and other

When it comes to shelf space, size is everything. With the range of scale models in production today, collectors can choose which scale they prefer. Although the 1/16 scale is the traditional size of most John Deere toys, other scales range from "Microsize" 1/128-scale models to massive 1/8-scale replicas. This Model B tractor from Ertl is shown in four sizes (from large to small): 1/8, 1/16, 1/32, and 1/64. *Nick Cedar*

foreign locales. Talented individuals known as "scratch-builders" have created hundreds of other John Deere scale models. These custom-built designs are very valuable due to the limited production numbers and the incredible detail.

It's easy to see the variety of sizes in farm toys (known as "scales") on the collectible market today. The original toy tractor size was 1/16 scale, meaning the full-size tractor is 16 times larger than the toy. By 1967, Ertl introduced the first 1/64-scale tractors. In the 1980s, designers at Ertl split the two scales to bring a 1/32 model to the European market. Not thinking 1/64 scale was quite tiny enough, Ertl went so far as to shrink the miniature into a 1/128 version called "Microsize" in 1990. The smaller the tractor, the more you can fit on a shelf, say most collectors. But that doesn't stop the Scale Models Company from building a 1/8-scale tractor, which is about the size of a small child.

Eventually, collectors find themselves narrowing their hobby to a particular scale, lest they run out of room with the multiple versions available. Other collectors choose to focus on a particular time frame, such as the two-cylinder era of 1923–1960. And some "purists" prefer to specialize in a particular manufacturer's line, such as Ertl.

Typically, a model licensed by Deere & Company holds more value than an unlicensed one. A closer study of a particular toy brings to light a multitude of variations for each model bearing the John Deere name. Look hard enough and you may discover the distinct differences as small as an extra hole for a spare rivet, a flat instead of a round alternator end, a shift lever, solid axle, tapered or straight air cleaner, or an alignment boss pin. There's even one variation that looks like a diesel engine on the right side, but has a gasoline engine on the left side! Once the error was discovered and a recall proved pointless, collectors owning this "mistake model" saw a tremendous increase in value from the "special" 3010 released in 1992.

In addition to toys, the entertainment category also includes bicycles, stuffed animals, even board games and playing cards… and all promote the John Deere brand in some way!

Farm Toy Production History

The earliest known farm toy production dates back to 1886, when James Wilkins first made a few 1/16-scale cast-iron models. Although Wilkins never made any John Deere equipment, he is credited with being the first to commercially produce farm toys in the United States.

The next major player in farm toy production surfaced in the 1920s when **Arcade Manufacturing Company** in Freeport, Illinois, began to produce cast-iron farm toys as a sideline business. Until the 1940s, Arcade made several farm toys for a number of brands, including a version of the styled John Deere Model A and a wagon running gear, both with rubber tires. However, the onset of World War II forced Arcade to save metal, and the company's toy production ended for good in 1942.

To cope with the Great Depression, the **National Sewing Machine Company** in Belvidere, Illinois, decided to diversify its production into the Vindex line of cast-iron toys and novelties, which included dog doorstops as well as miniature replicas of farm machinery. Unfortunately, the Depression took its toll and the company stopped making Vindex toys, leaving a legacy of now-very-valuable toys in its wake.

Modern farm toy production began after World War II's material restrictions for tin and iron were lifted. **Ertl**, perhaps the best-known name in farm toys, produced the first John Deere toy tractor in 1945 in the basement of the family home of Fred Ertl, Sr., in Dubuque, Iowa. Business boomed and manufacturing quickly outgrew Ertl's basement. In 1959, Ertl built a factory in Dyersville, Iowa, now home to the National Farm Toy Museum. To add stamped-steel implements to its product line, Ertl bought Carter Tru-Scale Products in 1971 and the "Structo" toy division in 1974. Soon after these acquisitions, Ertl began to export his creations, bringing John Deere green to the far-reaches of the world. Now considered the largest manufacturer of die-cast and steel models, Ertl continues to roll John Deere toys off the assembly line after an amazing history that spans more than 50 years and shows no signs of slowing any time soon.

The **Eska** business began in 1945 as the marketing arm for Ertl, shipping toys to John Deere dealerships across the United States. By 1948, Eska began making stamped-steel farm implements designed by the Carter Tru-Scale Company, which later acquired Eska and built toys under both brand names in the 1950s. Eska also made some of the earliest John Deere pedal tractors. Read more about these large sand-cast riding models later in the chapter.

Carter Tru-Scale is another popular name in farm toy manufacturing. Carter Machine and Tool Company first supplied stamped-steel toy implement components to the Eska Company in 1946. While founder Joe Carter actually designed most of the pieces marketed by Eska, he never took any credit until his company acquired Eska in 1950. Then Carter put his name on a 1/16-scale John Deere pressed-steel manure spreader with rubber tires. By 1965, he began to build Carter Tru-Scale farm toys, which represent fine craftsmanship to today's collectors. Carter became part of the Ertl holding company in 1971.

The **Spec-Cast Company** of Rockford, Illinois, started out making belt buckles in 1974. Later products included desk pen sets and other trophy-type items. After passing through several owners over a 10-year period, Spec-Cast began making farm toys in 1986. A 1/43-scale John Deere series from the 1990s included a farm truck, Waterloo Boy, Model AR, Model 730, and a Froelich tractor.

Considered by some to be a chip off the old block, Joe Ertl, son of Fred Ertl, Sr., turned his Dyersville Die Casting company into the **Scale Models** brand in 1978 after agreeing to a contract with White Farm Equipment. Products ranged from toy tractors and pedal tractors to model car kits, belt buckles, and other novelties. The company continues to be true to its roots as a small family-owned business doing what it loves. A recent line of 1/8-scale John Deere tractors has created quite a stir with collectors looking for great detail at an affordable price.

From the earliest Froelich, Dain, and Waterloo Boy tractors to the latest high-tech tracked marvels such as the 8000 and 9000 Series models, John Deere toys represent more than a century of tractor designs. The tractor was (and still is) the most popular toy on the market. Whether they have a narrow front end, cab, or duals, toy tractors still lead the collectible category. Some are steerable; others have rubber tires. A few have working three-point hitches, and recent versions can be found with remote control, electronic sounds, and other technological gadgets. Most tractors are driverless, although a few designs include a farmer figurine at the wheel. Design details clearly show the progression of time from the earlier, almost-crude versions to some of today's technically correct models.

With their intricate designs and tiny working parts, the "Precision Classics" Series from Ertl can amaze even the most skeptical. When displayed on a shelf next to a gold commemorative medallion, a Precision Classics scale model even impresses city slickers. A colorful carton and historical booklet are also included with each model.

Typically, a Special Edition or Collector's Model is released first. These toys are often more detailed and cost more than the shelf model that comes out later. An unbelievable number of special editions exist to mark various farm shows, toy shows, collector club events, manufacturing milestones, or agricultural organizations. Even gold-plated "trophy tractors" were awarded to dealers for meeting certain sales goals.

The distinct look of steel lug wheels, an aerodynamic orchard fender, or a tracked crawler version offer added appeal to collectors as well as attracting the attention of non-collectors. Skid-steer loaders, gasoline engines, the Dain three-wheeled tractor, and a snowmobile named Trailfire lengthen the list of unusual John Deere toys.

Even the lawn and garden line of John Deere tractors became "Ertl-ized" as a 1/64-scale model version of the 110 was produced in the early 1960s. Another interesting venture in 1969 involved lawn and garden tractors that weren't painted green. John Deere wanted to capitalize on the bright-color craze of the late 1960s, so it introduced a series of four tractors in Spruce Blue, Sunset Orange, Patio Red, and April Yellow with a Dogwood White chassis. Unfortunately, customers weren't as crazy about the rainbow quartet, and a two-year trial ended, leaving John Deere green as the preferred color of choice. Ertl's scale-model series and a special display version add an element of intrigue to any John Deere toy collection.

Other than that brief foray into other-colored paint, John Deere agricultural equipment and consumer products remain green with yellow accents. The only exception is the construction equipment division. These industrial models sport bright yellow paint with black accents. While the lack of green may not interest a diehard farm toy collector, John Deere's bulldozers, excavators, motor graders, wheel loaders, backhoes, and crawler tractors also earned the right to be immortalized by Ertl.

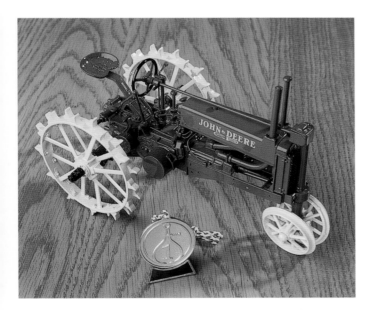

The "Precision Classics" series from Ertl began in 1990 with this unstyled Model A as its first edition. Equipped with steel wheels, this impressive replica of John Deere's 1934–1939 tractor design depicts a high degree of detail. Prices range from $125 in excellent condition to $275 for new in the box. *Nick Cedar*

The 1991 "Precision Classics" model is another unstyled Model A, but with rubber tires and a mounted Model 290 row-crop cultivator. The striking combination of the John Deere green tractor with the fire-engine-red accents of the cultivator makes a distinct presence on any shelf. This impressive scale model goes for $300 in excellent condition, or up to $600 for new in the box. *Nick Cedar*

Crawler tractors found popularity in both agricultural and industrial markets, so the first Model 40 crawler wore both green and yellow paint in the 1950s. The ag version (lower right) is a 1954 Model 40, while the yellow industrial one (upper left) is the 1959 Model 440. Note the styling differences between these two 1/16-scale models from Ertl. Take note that a front-mounted blade was offered with the Model 40, but not with the Model 440. These toys once belonged to William Hewitt, who served as the sixth president of Deere & Company from 1955 to 1982. *Nick Cedar*

The Model 430C crawler tractor was first built in 1958 as part of the 30 Series, the last of the two-cylinder tractors. The popular crawler came with four- or five-roller tracks in five different widths. The full-size 430 crawler offered clutch-brake steering, continuous-running PTO, optional direction reverser, and three-point hitch, along with a variety of additional options. This 1/16-scale model of the agricultural version made by Ertl in 1997 features excellent detail from the three-point hitch to the green metal cleats of the track. *Nick Cedar*

Deere & Company began to investigate the tractor market in 1912 when C. H. Melvin built the company's first experimental tractor. It didn't fare well in the field and was soon scrapped entirely. But Deere's entry into tractor manufacturing was inevitable, and the company gave the task of designing the next one to Joe Dain. In 1918, 100 models of his All-Wheel Drive tractor made manufacturing history. Dain's goal was to design a tractor that could be sold for $700, but his effort ended up costing twice that. The All-Wheel Drive design was ahead of its time for many reasons, including its ability to change speeds without stopping the tractor. This 1/16-scale model with plastic chain was manufactured by Scale Models of Dyersville, Iowa, for the 1996 Aftermarket Expo in Nashville. A reprint of the original 1919 sales leaflet was included the model. *Nick Cedar*

A few years after the Waterloo Boy purchase, John Deere introduced the Model D tractor in 1923. Early versions from 1924 to 1925 were known as a "spoker D" because of the spoked flywheel. The solid flywheel design started in 1926. This 1930s cast-iron 1/16-scale toy by Vindex is green with yellow wheels and features a nickel-plated driver and pulley. Valued around $2,000 today, the original probably sold for about $1 during the Depression. *Denny Eilers*

Soon after the Dain All-Wheel Drive design was released, Deere inherited the Waterloo Boy two-cylinder tractor line by buying the Waterloo Gasoline Engine Company of Waterloo, Iowa, in March 1918. The radiator of this 1/16-scale model from Ertl in 1988 bears this inscription: "Special Edition Model "R" Waterloo Boy 1914-1919." A shelf version has a screen decal on the radiator instead. *Nick Cedar*

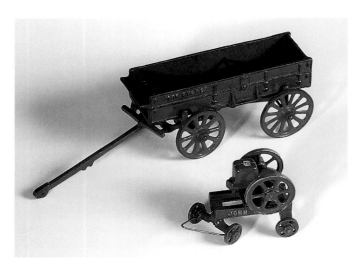

Built during the Great Depression, Vindex cast-iron toys made by the National Sewing Machine Company represent the earliest versions of John Deere farm equipment. This wagon and stationary engine in 1/16 scale are scarce farm toys and can each bring from $500 to $2,000 today. *Denny Eilers*

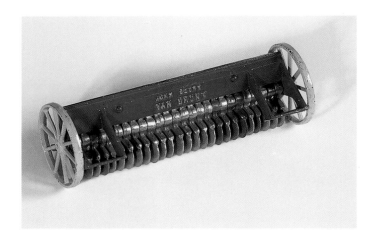

Admired for its fine detail, this 1930s Vindex 1/16-scale toy of a John Deere-Van Brunt grain drill measures almost 10 inches long and features individual discs for each row. *Denny Eilers*

A toy collector's dream would be to own one of the first three 1/16-scale tractor models made in the basement of the Ertl family home back in 1945. This Model A with the cast driver, rubber tires, and closed flywheel represents the third major edition released in 1947. Three variations with a few subtle differences are known to exist. This one has the words "Ertl Toy" cast on the bottom of the steering post on either side, as well as a molded pattern in the front tires. Wayne Eisele, a Deere & Company employee, designed the attached loader in the 1950s. His first design mounted on the front frame of the tractor and wrapped around the rear axles. The bucket arms raised and lowered with the crank, while a trip lever on the left side of the bucket gave it dumping action. This toy has been customized with the John Deere decal and the chain (the original was a string). *Nick Cedar*

Arcade built these two 1/16-scale replicas of the John Deere Model A in the 1940s. A nickel-plated driver is at the helm of this cast-iron version with rubber tires. Yellow-centered wheels accent the green paint on the tractor body. Some models even have silver highlight paint on the pulley and magneto-distributor. These 1941 toys represent the 1938-styled Model A. Note the Arcade logo emblem at the driver's feet on the rear model. *Denny Eilers*

Deere & Company began to develop its first row-crop tractor in 1926, which led to a tricycle-type design in 1928. With steel lug rear wheels and dish-type wheels on a narrow front end, this 1/16-scale replica from Ertl represents a 1929 General Purpose Wide Tread (GPWT) tractor. Note the offset seat of this side-steer design to give the operator a better view of the rows. Over-hood steering was added to the GPWT tractors in 1932. Both standard and side-steer models went through four styles: one had no air cleaner stack or exhaust through the hood (shown); another had the air stack on the right-hand side; the third variation had an air stack through the hood; and the last one had two vertical stacks. *Nick Cedar*

Ertl produced these two 1/16-scale replicas of the John Deere Model A in the 1940s. The 1946 toy tractor in the foreground is believed to be the second version made in the Ertl basement. It features a cast-in driver, open-style flywheel, and rubber tires. Note the absence of a steering post, plus the casting "web" between the exhaust and air cleaner stacks. One known variation is the presence of headlights over the flywheel. The other toy tractor represents the third version from 1947, signified by a closed flywheel and separate steering post. A few variations of this model exist, so consult a toy guide for full details. In the 1980s, a special edition of the Model A was released to celebrate Ertl's 40th anniversary (1945–1985). *Denny Eilers*

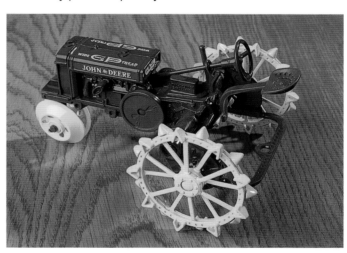

These two toy tractors represent experimental designs that were never officially produced as toys or the real McCoys. See how the driver sits over the front wheels rather than toward the rear? This could be an attempt to improve visibility, especially in row crops, given that the tricycle-type tractor was under development in the 1920s. While not identical to a specific model, these toys are most similar to the GP tricycle, GPWT, and the Model P built from 1928 to 1931. The bottom toy resembles an Arcade model because of its nickel-plated driver at the wheel. The rear version does not appear to be complete, but note its larger size and different wheels and tires. Both are wood models with rubber tires. *Denny Eilers*

This John Deere Model G 1/16-scale toy tractor celebrates the influence of the Iowa Future Farmers of America, an agricultural youth organization. This 1999 Special Edition includes the FFA logo as a decal on the tractor, a special FFA awning, and the young girl (sculpted by Lowell Davis) at the wheel. *Nick Cedar*

Built between 1947 and 1952, the Model M was an ideal small utility tractor for a variety of chores on the farm. This 1/16-scale toy from 1986 is the third model in Ertl's historical series. Two versions are known to exist—the collector edition features a cast inscription with the words "Dubuque 1946-1952, Model M, Series III" on the lower left frame and an Ertl mark on the right. *Nick Cedar*

The Model 60 LPG Orchard tractor from 1957 sports sleek, aerodynamic fender shields to protect the tractor and operator from branches and vines. With a wide front end and rubber tires, this toy was released for the 1993 John Deere Aftermarket Expo in Nashville. A collector insert with Customer Roundup logo and special collector carton accompany this Ertl 1/16-scale model. Oddly enough, Deere & Company only built about 50 of the full-size tractors. Billed as an economical alternative to gasoline/diesel fuel, Liquefied Petroleum Gas (LPG) tractors found popularity in the 1950s and 1960s in areas where natural gas was abundant. The fuel tank was much larger because LPG required pressurized storage to prevent evaporation. *Nick Cedar*

In honor of its 1990 Expo II show, the Two-Cylinder Club contracted Ertl to make 10,000 toy tractors patterned after the Model 720 Hi-Crop built from 1956 to 1958. A special carton and engraving on the left side of the frame distinguish this 1/16 version from a later collector model (Special Edition 1990). These "stilt-type" tractors offered extra clearance under the frame to help farmers spray or cultivate larger crops in later stages. *Nick Cedar*

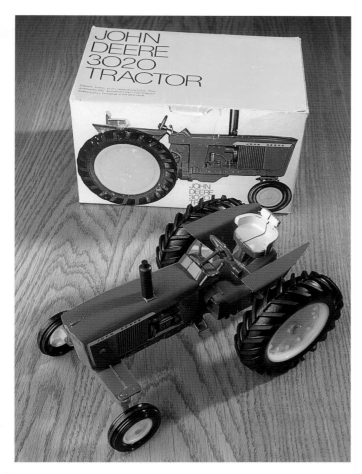

The Model 3020 Diesel is a very popular replica from Ertl's New Generation 1/16-scale John Deere tractors. This 1964 toy represents a wide front-axle model made from 1964 to 1968. Note the dash levers and other details. Apparently, some boxes were misnamed as 4020s. Study a specific toy collector's guide to determine details and dates for each variation. *Nick Cedar*

This 1/16-scale Ertl toy represents the Model 5020 Diesel standard with a wide front end, one of the New Generation tractors built from 1966 to 1972. The toy 5020 holds the honor of the longest production run (1969–1992) for an Ertl model. Naturally, numerous variations result from a long production run. These variations can be found in the air cleaners, axle braces, and dash levers. Some special editions also exist. This 1969 version still has its original box, adding $100 to its value. *Nick Cedar*

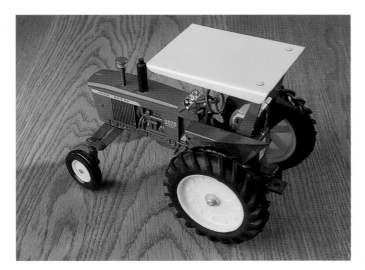

This 3020 with ROPS canopy represents a 1969–1972 model. Note the air cleaner and absence of a three-point hitch. Many variations of the popular Model 3020 exist today, so consult a toy collecting guide for full details. Some differences include a narrow or wide front, with or without a three-point hitch, bolt-on or riveted-on ROPS, dash levers, tires, Power Shift transmission, oil filters, and alternator. *Nick Cedar*

Representing a new line of four-wheel drive tractors introduced in 1972, Ertl produced the articulated John Deere Model 7520 as a 1/16-scale toy. A major variation involves the air cleaner—none, straight one-piece, or tapered two-piece (shown). *Nick Cedar*

While not the major focus of farm toy collecting, John Deere implements still make up a significant segment of the market. Primary pieces of equipment on a farm of the past include a plow to till the soil, a planter to sow the seeds, and a combine to harvest the crop. The loader tractor and wagon were also considered indispensable tools on the farm.

Plowing Planet Earth

From his blacksmith shop in Grand Detour, Illinois, a young John Deere invented a self-cleaning plow that could turn over the sticky soils of the midwestern prairie. News of the plow's success spread quickly and sales rose accordingly. No other image—except for the leaping deer—can be considered a more recognizable icon for Deere & Company. John Deere's famed design of 1837 led to the growth of a company now revered as a worldwide leader in farm equipment manufacturing.

From the walking plow to modern multi-bottom tractor-towed units, the plow has seen significant innovations since its invention in 1837. Plow designs changed to match the growing horsepower in tractors of the time. Early two-bottom units made way for three-, four-, five-, and even six-bottom plows in trailing, semi-mounted, and three-point hitch versions. Today, plows are not as popular in

many areas due to the no-till and reduced-till movements that encourage farmers to limit their tillage operations to as few as possible.

The first scale-model plow was made in the 1930s under the Vindex brand name. Few are known to exist, and values are estimated at $2,000. Eska-Carter released several scale-model versions during the 1950s. Ertl built John Deere toy plows in the 1960s, and Sigomec built several versions in the 1970s.

Sowing the Seeds that Feed

Early mechanical planting efforts made the springtime task less labor-intensive. What used to take several rounds with a two-row horse-drawn planter now takes just one

Known for superior traction and reduced soil compaction, crawler tractors fit a special niche in agricultural and industrial markets. In a joint venture with Lindeman Manufacturing of Yakima, Washington, John Deere built the Model BO-L crawler from 1943 to 1946. Dubuque Works made the Model MC crawler from 1948 until 1952, and the Model 40 crawler in 1953. Ertl manufactured a miniature version of the Model 40 with rubber tracks in 1954. In addition to the green-and-yellow ag model, a yellow-and-black industrial version also exists. An optional front-mounted blade was available for the ag version only. This tracked tractor is shown pulling a two-bottom moldboard plow, also built by Eska-Carter in the early 1950s. This ribbed-tire version features an adjusting lever and sprocket in place of an earlier hand-crank design. These toys once belonged to William Hewitt. *Nick Cedar*

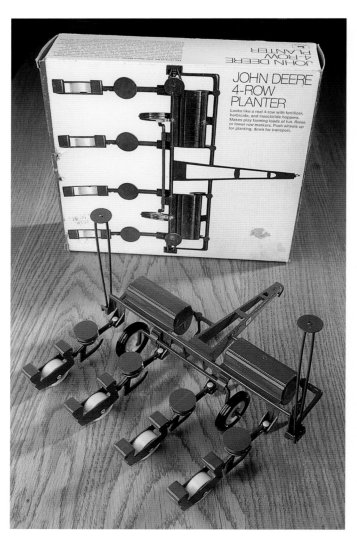

A John Deere four-row planter in 1/16 scale from Ertl matches the popular Model 494 planter. This 1965 toy was made for 10 years, leaving several variations in design details. Differences in the row markers, hitch tongue, coulter shank, and decals distinguish the varying models. As the original box touts, "Looks like a real 4-row with fertilizer, herbicide and insecticide hoppers. Makes play farming loads of fun. Raise or lower row markers. Push wheels up for planting, down for transport." *Nick Cedar*

pass with today's tractor-drawn planter models that cover up to 31 rows at a time.

The early wooden Deere & Mansur rotary-drop corn planter evolved into the No. 9 edge-drop, then the No. 999, which could handle several seed types. While John Deere planters had been sowing seeds for more than 50 seasons, a scale model wasn't made until 1965 when Ertl released a 1/16-scale four-row planter. This popular toy, patterned after the Model 494, was manufactured for a decade, resulting in numerous variations.

Later models grew in size until the famed MaxEmerge® row-unit system revolutionized planting in 1974. Ertl released a 1/16-scale version of the Model 7000 in 1975 with plastic fertilizer, seed, and herbicide boxes. The MaxEmerge 2 design came out in 1985, followed by Ertl's first 1/64-scale replica. Since 1996, John Deere planters have worn the MaxEmergePlus decal. Farmers worldwide have come to respect the MaxEmerge name for planting accuracy.

Grain drills entered the John Deere line of farm equipment in 1911 when the famous Van Brunt models were acquired. Van Brunt was synonymous with quality seeding equipment, and the name remained on John Deere grain drills until 1957. The oldest of all toy drills is the 1930s Vindex replica with red box, yellow wheels, and silver discs. This model is one of the most sought-after, and is valued around $4,000 today. Carter Tru-Scale made a highly detailed version in the early 1950s. Variations include green or yellow lids and green or unpainted disks. In 1989, Ertl released a 1/16-scale John Deere 452 grain drill and a 1/64-scale model John Deere 8300 grain drill with detachable

press wheels. Other John Deere scale-model drills came from Terry Rouch and Standi Toys.

Harvesting Gets a Helping Hand

The joint effort of a reaper and a thresher resulted in a combine, a modern grain harvester introduced in the early 1900s. Early horse-drawn models gave way to self-propelled models, which are primarily used on farms today. Considered by some to be the most sought-after John Deere toy, the 1930s Vindex version of an early prairie combine tips the scales at 11 pounds due to its cast-iron construction.

John Deere's first combines were introduced in 1927. The popular model No. 12A with its left-hand cut sold 116,000 units during its 13-year manufacturing run starting in 1940. The toy version came out in 1950 from Eska-Carter. By 1947, Deere introduced its first self-propelled model, the No. 55. Over the 22 years of its production, nearly 84,000 units were sold. A special self-leveling version (Model 55H) came out in 1954 to revolutionize harvesting in the rolling hills of the Pacific Northwest.

In 1970, Ertl entered the toy combine market with the die-cast Model 6600 in a slightly smaller 1/24 scale. Ertl built the Titan Series combines in 1978 followed by the Titan II in 1987. Titan combines were even designed down to a minuscule 1/50 scale by Ertl in the 1980s. The 9500 and 9600 combines became 1/28-scale model replicas from Ertl in 1989. Late-model John Deere combines and their scale replicas came complete with multiple heads for grain and corn. Introduced in 1999, the 50 Series STS combine marks the newest model from John Deere.

John Deere introduced the Model No. 12A in 1940. A decade later, this scale model was made by Carter Tru-Scale and marketed by Eska. These two companies would later merge into the Ertl Company. Introduced in the early 1950s, the 1/16-scale model features chain-driven gears that drive the reel and cloth "canvas" conveyor. A sticker on the top gave oiling instructions for the toy, although it's very rare to find the sticker still intact. A collector's edition was released in 1990 to mark the 50th anniversary of the 12A combine. This vintage toy once belonged to William Hewitt. *Nick Cedar*

In 1970, Ertl entered the scale-model combine market with this die-cast Model 6600 for John Deere. Unlike the traditional 1/16 scale, this model was a slightly smaller 1/24 scale. Manufactured by Ertl for 10 years, this 6600 was a popular toy with young John Deere fans. Note the center drive chain for the auger and a gear drive for the reel on this 1974 variation. Today, this model in mint condition might fetch around $200; new in the box could be worth $350. In 1978, the metal reel and bat boards were replaced with plastic. *Nick Cedar*

Types of Tools Found on Farms of All Sizes

The tractor-mounted loader and wagon, perhaps the most active pair on the farm, served a multitude of purposes all year round. The productive team could carry grain, haul hay bales, feed cattle, move snow, or take the family to town.

While the essential concept behind a wagon is still intact in today's designs, newer models have advanced features beyond a basic box and running gear. The self-unloading forage wagon (or chuck wagon), the gravity box for grain, high-sided hay bale wagon, and the hydraulic dump wagon represent significant innovations in wagon engineering.

The front-end loader saved farmers from back-breaking labor like lifting dirt, rock, manure, seed, feed, and fertilizer around farms and fields. An ideal partner for a John Deere tractor, loaders were one of the more complex scale models on the market in the 1950s.

Other popular implements turned into toys include disk harrows, cultivators, grain drills, hay rakes, manure spreaders, mower conditioners, and sprayers. A variety of John Deere vehicles were also manufactured in miniature, such as tractor trailers, service trucks, and other types of dealer transportation.

While not quite as popular as toy tractors, matching scale model implements add another dimension of enjoyment when "playing farm." All three of these implements are early 1950s designs from Eska-Carter. Lower left: Model L manure spreader with front adjustment levers and cleated tires. Middle right: Early 1950s "drag" or "pull" tandem disk (disk harrow without transport wheels). Excellent detail ranges from adjustable gangs and rolling disk blades to a latch mechanism to set gang angle. Top: The first model square baler features unpainted pick-up teeth, flattened axle ends, an L-shaped hitch on the tongue, and no rear wagon hitch. Early style decals (yellow letters on black) with ribbed tires round out other key details. Every hay baler toy came with tiny plastic bales—many of which were likely devoured by pets or misplaced by children. These toys once belonged to William Hewitt. *Nick Cedar*

Ertl produced this 1/16-scale toy disk harrow in the late 1950s. This four-gang tandem drag-type disk includes a flattened axle end as one variation and a push-nut as another. Note the crank-type hitch and die-cast wheels. The accompanying box displays a grinning young man ready "for more indoor and outdoor fun!" *Nick Cedar*

The John Deere Model 60 replaced the Model B in 1952. As the first steerable John Deere Ertl, this 1/16-scale toy from 1955 features "step-down" axles for securing a mounted loader, as shown here. If there's a hole underneath the toy tractor, it was probably a drain hole for excess paint. Note the cast work light on the back of the seat. The matching front loader (Model 45) from Eska-Carter mounts over the rear axles and is secured by a clamp under the engine. The complex 1950s design included multiple hinges, levers, and springs to give the loader its lift and dump capability. These toys once belonged to William Hewitt. *Nick Cedar*

The mechanical Model 227 corn picker mounted to the Model 60 tractor made quick work of harvesting corn, especially compared to the labor-intensive alternative of picking by hand. Early corn pickers were often mounted directly to the tractor, while others were pull-type designs. In 1952, Eska-Carter manufactured a miniature "short nose" version to fit the steerable Model 60, as well as the 620 and 630 tractors. One version uses a different style decal while another 1961 "longer nosed" scale model fits the 3010–3020 tractor style. The elevator carries the corn up and into the trailing flare wagon. This early 1950s 1/16-scale model wagon from Eska-Carter was made of stamped steel. A removable box, steerable running gear, and an adjustable tailgate can be found on all versions. A one-piece tongue and small solid-rubber tires make this version distinct. Others sport different tires and a two-piece tongue steering mechanism. The decals also varied from model to model. These toys once belonged to William Hewitt. *Nick Cedar*

The first, and perhaps most famous, John Deere pedal tractor was not even an official version. A John Deere Model A riding tractor made by Eska in 1949 is now nicknamed the "coffin block" for its incorrect engine shape showing a long, rectangular four-cylinder engine instead of a shorter two-cylinder one. Apparently, the 10 models made for salesman samples are all that remain of the manufacturing mistake. These Eska pedal tractors were actually painted red and had no John Deere identification. Despite the fact that Deere never approved these "coffin block" models, these unique pedal tractors can bring up to $20,000 due to their extremely rare existence and unusual history. Marketed by Eska in 1950, the first "official" John Deere Model A pedal tractor looks almost identical to the "coffin block" version, except for the engine shape, of course. While it's not the "mistake model," this original edition still brings about $5,000.

After the first Model A by Eska, pedal tractors patterned after the Model 60 (small and large), the 620, and the 730 tractors were released in the late 1950s. Then came the 10 (3010) and 20 (3020) models in the early 1960s. The LGT, 4430, 4440, and 4450 models were built in the 1970s–1980s. Ertl released an industrial pedal tractor in 1990, followed by the 4020 Diesel in 1991, the 7600 in 1995, the 7410 in 1997, and the 8400 in 1999. Today, pedal tractors from the 1950s and 1960s bring around $1,000, 1970s models are around $500, and the 1980s–1990s versions might be valued at approximately $250.

As the largest scale-model replicas available, pedal tractors vary slightly in size from the 34-inch original models up to the larger 38-inch models. Another unique aspect of pedal tractors is accessories such as two-wheel trailers and even umbrella canopies. A study of pedal tractor parts quickly overwhelms even the most interested collector, as the variety of wheels and tires, hubcaps, push nuts, seats, steering wheels, axles, chains, pedals, and even hitch bolts make for a very lengthy list. Now, consider the number of available options due to customization, such as decals, levers, lights, fenders, and gauges. These realistic parts and pieces add a whole new dimension to these "rideable" miniature model tractors.

Originally intended for children's entertainment, pedal tractors now also participate in pulling contests across the country. Large crowds gather to cheer on the drivers who must pedal hard enough to move the weighted sled the farthest on the track. Today's pedal tractor pulls enjoy an almost cultlike following, which proves that these tractors aren't just for kids!

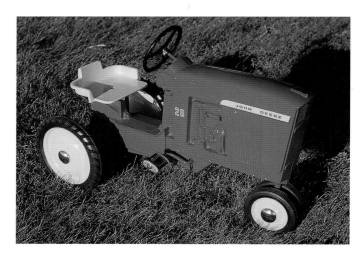

The Model 20 was the first pedal tractor manufactured and marketed by Ertl. This variation came out in 1965 and is distinguished from the earlier 1963 edition by its smooth dome-type rim instead of a star-patterned wheel. *Nick Cedar*

Ertl made a special Lawn and Garden Tractor (LGT) in 1970. The first to feature a wide front axle, this pedal tractor also sports fenders, smooth rear tires, and high-back seat, making it distinctly different from its farm tractor counterparts. *Nick Cedar*

Granted, scale-model toy tractors and implements constitute the largest segment of John Deere memorabilia designed for children. But a variety of other entertaining pieces also exists, including stuffed animals, puzzles, board games, playing cards, marbles, baseball bats, golf clubs, and even bicycles.

These diverse items are often the target of unlicensed creations or dealer-approved versions, because Deere & Company did not officially produce or authorize many of them. Collectors must take care in adding such items to their collections. Whether it's an airplane, car, snowmobile, or race car, research its history first and pay according to its authenticity.

Considering the marketability for such collectibles, some people are targeting John Deere collectors with fake memorabilia. These scam artists have even gone to great lengths to create seemingly legitimate proof that their "fantasy" items are officially "authentic" or "vintage." When it comes to marbles and some of the other "popular and pricey" collectibles, it's buyer beware!

John Deere's Horicon Works manufactured nearly 225,000 snowmobiles from 1971 to 1982. An "Enduro Team Deere" racing team won acclaim with the Liquidator and Liquifire models. Other race-inspired sleds were named Cyclone, Sportfire, Sprintfire, and Trailfire. Normatt built this plastic 1/10-scale replica of the Model 400 in 1972. *Denny Eilers*

Considered an almost secret part of John Deere history, the Deere-Clark automobile represents a short-term manufacturing venture from the early 1900s. These 1907 cars were made at the factory of the Deere-Clark Motor Car Company in East Moline. Back then, a fully equipped brand-new car cost $2,500. These 1/20-scale models from Joseph F. Murphy, Inc., also included a reprint of the original catalog for the Type "B" two-seater (1992) and Type "C" Gentleman's Roadster (1993). The Type C car sports bright red paint with black accents and even a brown plastic luggage trunk in the rear. Deep purple paint, black trim, and gold-plated accents give the Type B two-seater a distinct presence. Both models ride on white balloon-type rubber tires. A special gold-plated model served as a dealer sales incentive, resulting in limited quantities and therefore, higher collectible values. *Nick Cedar*

In the early 1900s, Dain Manufacturing Company of Ottumwa, Iowa, built "Commercial Cars." The original three-ton trucks used a friction transmission and direct drive design to revolutionize forward and reverse speeds. This 1/16-scale model of a Dain "Parts Express" truck was designed by Joseph F. Murphy, Inc., and manufactured by the Scale Models Company of Dyersville, Iowa. Approximately 11,000 were sold at the 1989 Aftermarket Conference & Parts Expo in Nashville. *Denny Eilers*

John Deere Bicycles

Around the same time that buggies and wagons were in their heyday, the bicycle craze caught the attention of Mr. Webber and Mr. Velie at the Minneapolis branch. In the mid-1890s, Deere & Webber marketed two outside brands plus three company-branded models—the Deere Leader, the Deere Roadster, and the Moline Special. In August 1895, the branch sponsored the "Deere Road Race" over a 20-mile course at Lake Harriet near Minneapolis. The Kansas City and Omaha branches soon joined in the sales efforts, too. Velie even developed a special trademark with a deer riding a bicycle. An 1899 product catalog featuring the "FAWN" and "REINDEER" models announced, "We are in the bicycle business to remain, and the purchaser of one of our Bicycles is assured that he will be well cared for through the life of his mount." Despite that bold statement, the bicycle basically rode itself out of business by 1900 until Deere & Company briefly revisited bicycle manufacturing in the 1970s. From 1972 to 1976, Deere sold more than 200,000 made-in-Taiwan bicycles including 20-inch boys' and girls' Hi-Rise models, 26-inch men's and women's 3-speeds, and 27-inch 10-speeds.

This ad for bicycles from Deere & Webber graced the back cover of *The Furrow* magazine in 1897. Note the trademark logo, deer on bicycle symbol, and railcars for "Deere Vehicles." *Nick Cedar*

These bicycles supposedly belonged to the William Hewitt family in the 1970s. Hewitt was president of Deere & Company from 1955 to 1982. The green three-speed women's model and the yellow banana-seat girl's bike were built between 1972 and 1975. *Nick Cedar*

This bicycle represents one of the models built in the late 1890s by Minneapolis branch Deere & Webber. This men's model sold for $40 to $50 when new in 1900. Because few of these vintage bicycles with wooden wheels are known to exist, prices run between $1,000 and $2,500 on today's collectible market. One model has been seen with an early headlight contraption—a lantern mounted on the front axle. *Denny Eilers*

Certainly an eye-catcher, this figurine of a deer riding a bicycle represents the Deere bicycle trademark designed by Charles Velie for Deere & Webber in the late 1890s. Joseph F. Murphy, Inc., manufactured a limited number of these 5-inch-high miniature die-cast replicas as a special promotion for the Aftermarket & Parts Expo. The base is inscribed with the "JD CUSTOMER ROUNDUP" logo and "NASHVILLE 1993." A special gold-plated model was also available to dealers who ordered a certain quantity for resale. *Nick Cedar*

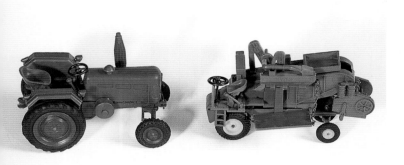

An intricately detailed plastic combine model represents a John Deere-Lanz version made around 1960. German manufacturer Rex scaled this miniature to approximately 1/43 scale. Unlike traditional auger-unloading combines, this self-propelled combine uses a grain bagger. A tiny chain allows the bagging platform to be raised or lowered. This model is missing the yellow rails that protect the attendant on the bagging platform, as well as the grain head with reel and auger. Rex also made the plastic 1/21-scale Lanz Bulldog tractor with wide front end in 1959. Several color combinations were released, including this blue body with red wheels. Values can reach $700 per toy as collectibles today. *Denny Eilers*

The original edition of the John Deere Farm Game was released in 1938 from the John Deere Plow Company. The Omaha branch mailed this game to a customer in Essex, Iowa. The "Master Farmer" game was also reproduced in 1998 to honor its 50th anniversary. Prices for the original board game (16x20 inches) with spinners and all eight markers range from $50 in good condition to $250 for new in the box. *Nick Cedar*

For John Deere collectors, a deer is probably the most appropriate stuffed animal to add to a collection. Tagged "Little Johnny Dearest," a stuffed deer made by the B. J. Toy Company was marketed through John Deere dealers in the early- and mid-1980s. This green-and-yellow version has a brown-and-tan twin—each measures approximately 14 inches tall. *Nick Cedar*

John Deere Motorsports gave the green light to enter the NASCAR league in 1996 with Chad Little driving the #23 Grand Prix car on the Busch Series/Grand National Division racing circuit. In 1997, Deere teamed up with Roush Racing to sponsor Little in a #97 Ford on the Winston Cup circuit. The "John Deere green" car and crew always strived to cross the finish line first with the wave of the checkered flag. This large 1/18-scale replica of the #23 new in the box from Ertl joins a 1/64-scale replica of the #97 car still in the package with collector card and display stand. Today, the larger car brings $100 at auction, while the small toy can be found for around $40. *Brenda Kruse*

Considered to be America's favorite pastime, the sport of baseball was used to promote John Deere, too. The Louisville Slugger Little League bat with gold lettering has never touched a baseball's seams. On a recent auction, this bat brought $160 by itself. The John Deere Credit baseball imprinted with logo and "Building Your Business" slogan hit a homerun when it was used as a promotional item. *Brenda Kruse*

John Deere didn't leave out the "little folks" from its promotional efforts. Two storybooks illustrated by Roy A. Bostrom were first released in 1958 and 1959. *Johnny Tractor and His Pals,* written by Louise Price Bell, and *Corny Cornpicker Finds a Home,* written by Lois Zortman Hobbs, delighted young readers with colorful artwork and enchanting tales. Today, prices range from $25 to $75 depending on condition. Reproductions of these two plus two new storybooks were released in the late 1980s. John Deere also created several coloring books over the years. This one is from 1969 and came with a box of four crayons. *Nick Cedar*

John Deere Buggies and Wagons

John Deere was only in the buggy business for 25 years (1899–1923) and built wood wagons for 40 years (1907–1947). Nonetheless, these products represent some of the earliest engineering marketed by Deere & Company.

The Mansur & Tebbetts Implement Company started selling buggies as early as 1883. By 1891, the St. Louis sales branch had sold enough buggies, carriages, and surreys to warrant a separate vehicle factory to build a line marketed as "White Elephant Vehicles." Deere & Company officially purchased the buggy line in 1899 and incorporated the factory as the John Deere Reliance Buggy Company in 1913.

The Omaha sales branch of Deere, Wells & Company also carried another line of vehicles made by the Velie Carriage Company of Moline, which was founded in 1900 by Willard Velie, a grandson of John Deere. Velie worked for Deere from 1890 to 1900 and served on its board of directors until 1921.

In 1923, Deere chose to drop its line of buggies to concentrate on farm equipment, which included wood and steel wagons. Over the years, the John Deere wagon line included models such as "The Mitchell," "Old Hickory," "Ironclad," and "Triumph."

As early as 1881, John Deere's St. Louis and Kansas City branches sold wood wagons to customers making their westward migration to California. By 1912, Deere owned the three manufacturers who supplied these wood wagons—Fort Smith (Arkansas) Wagon Company, Moline (Illinois) Wagon Company, and Davenport (Iowa) Wagon Company. Deere bought the Fort Smith Wagon Company in 1907 and moved production to Moline in 1925. Deere purchased the Moline Wagon Company in 1910 and renamed it the John Deere Wagon Company, which became the Wagon Works in 1913. Deere also acquired the Roller Bearing Steel Wagon line from Davenport Wagon Company in 1911. By 1917, Deere consolidated the line at the Wagon Works. This factory flourished during World War I but faltered after World War II when farmers chose steel wagons with rubber tires. Production of wood wagons ceased in 1947.

An 1899 product catalog from the John Deere Plow Company of Kansas City promoted the Reliance buggy line along with Deere bicycles. The catalog boasted "We Laugh at Competition." Detailed illustrations of the available products accompanied specifications and prices. The 4200 Reliance (shown on the left) sold for $100 back then. *Brenda Kruse*

Light enough to be pulled by goats or large dogs, this miniature wooden wagon offered hours of fun for children on the farm long before the advent of dirt bikes and four-wheelers. Modeled after the full-size antique-style wagons found on every farm in the early 1900s, John Deere marketed its first "Junior Wagon" around 1912. The wagon box is 42 inches long and 30 inches high to the top of the seat. Sears, Roebuck and Company sold a non-John Deere version as early as 1908 for $4.73. In the 1980s, Deere released a reproduction version (shown) with cast-aluminum wheels and a 35-inch long wagon box standing 31 inches high. *Nick Cedar*

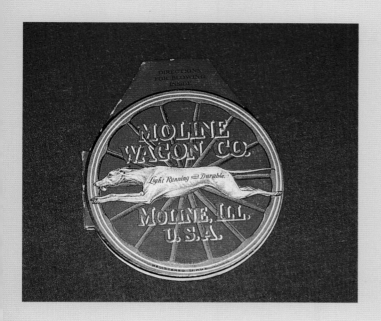

James First, who once worked as a blacksmith for John Deere, returned to his wheelwright trade in 1854 when he established the Moline Wagon Company. First incorporated the business in 1869 along with partners Morris Rosenfield and Charles Benser. In 1881, Rosenfield bought a one-third interest in Deere, Wells & Company in Omaha, Nebraska, which allowed the Moline wagons to be sold at John Deere branches. Deere & Company bought the Moline Wagon Company in 1910. This cardboard-type whistle promotes the fact that more than 1 million "Moline" wagons were on farms across the world. Named the "Loud Ad," this whistle was patented on April 20, 1909. Some of the text inside reads: "This world is a great deal of 'BLOW.' One advantage we enjoy is that others BLOW for us; Every man who has used one is blowing the merits and the many good features of the 'Moline Wagon'—Light Running and Durable—like a Grey Hound." *Brenda Kruse*

To honor Deere's history of buggy and wagon production, these two 1/16-scale models were designed by Joseph F. Murphy, Inc. and manufactured by Scale Models. The antique wagon replica was built for the 1989 Aftermarket Conference & Parts Expo in Nashville. A total of 7,000 were made and sold to dealers for $11.50 each. The Reliance Buggy was sold to dealers at the 1990 Parts Expo in Phoenix. At a selling price of $16.25 each, 20,000 models were built. *Denny Eilers*

Appendix A: Value Guides

In most situations involving antiques or collectibles, price guides must always be prefaced with a disclaimer that reminds the reader of the unpredictable nature of the market. This one is no different. Unlike commodities, collectibles have no standard pricing structure or established range of reasonable value. The following value guides are provided purely as examples for general reference and information.

The prices listed are for items pictured in this book and are estimated ranges established by several collectors and auctioneers. The range may represent an approximate average for what the market might bear. Do not depend on the low or high number as a bargaining tool in buying or selling a certain piece. Remember to consider the collectible's condition and authenticity (or origin) when setting or accepting a price.

The author does not claim any authority in dispensing advice on the legal aspects of a collecting hobby such as tax liability or insurance coverage. When values of John Deere memorabilia are required for a hobby or a business, please consult appropriate professionals for guidance with these issues.

Item	Remarks	Date	Value Range
Chapter 2			
Watch Fobs:			
Mother of Pearl shield/leaping deer	Antlers forward/open space	1910–1940	$150–300
Mother of Pearl shield/leaping deer	Antlers backward/filled space	1910–1940	150–300
Mother of Pearl shield/plow	Larger/John Deere on plow	1910–1940	250–600
Centennial round bronze	John Deere bust/prairie schooner	1937	50–250
Centennial round bronze	John Deere bust/centennial	1937	50–250
Black oval/leaping deer over plow	Colored enamel background	1910–1940	400–900
Royal blue oval/leaping deer over plow	Colored enamel background	1910–1940	250–500
Turquoise powder blue oval/leaping deer	Colored enamel background	1910–1940	250–500
Red, white & blue oval/leaping deer	Colored enamel background	1910–1940	300–550
Black shield/sunburst	"Trademark" wording	1930–1940	150–250
Waterloo Boy	Pewter	1920s	400–600
Model D tractor	Celluloid color on gold-plated	1920s	600–1,500
Bronze four-legged leaping deer	1956 trademark reproduction	1980s	50–100
Round coin-like leaping deer over plow	John Deere bust on back	1910s	600–1,500
Bronze shield shape/Butts Building	"Plows/Velie Buggies" wording	1920s	300–400
1876 logo with color	"Strongsville, Ohio" wording	1995	15–45
Moline Wagon running dog/wheel	Silver or gold-plated	1910s	150–300
Moline Wagon running dog/wheel	Black with red accents/no words	1910s	150–300
Velie round pewter spoked wheel	Velie in blue on white	1920s	100–250
Velie round silver	"The Name Ensures The Quality"	1920s	150–250
Velie large letter "V" shape	White letters w/ scrollwork	1920s	200–300
Velie smaller letter "V" shape	Yellow letters	1920s	200–300
Dain dangling celluloid pin	With color/Dain dog	1890–1910	150–300
Dain celluloid spinner fob	With color/Carrollton, Mo.	1890–1910	150–300
Deere & Mansur silver oval key fob	Large rack/wording on back	1890–1910	200–400
Pins/buttons:			
Gold-plated deer leaping over plow	Antlers backward/open space	1910–1940	10–40
Gold-plated deer leaping over plow	Antlers backward/filled space/on card	1910–1940	20–60
Gold-plated small shield	"John Deere Plow Co. St. Louis Mo."	1910s	200–500
Waterloo Boy	Boy with hat	1910s	100–150
Plow	"Syracuse" on the share	1910s	50–150
Great Dain pinback	Red with gold lettering	1910s	125–175
Deere & Mansur ear of corn	"Corn Planters" 1907 trademark	1910s	100–150
Moline Wagon spoked wheel/greyhound	"Thick" version	1890–1910	50–75
Moline Wagon spoked wheel/greyhound	"Thin" version	1890–1910	75–125
Dangling celluloid John Deere Plows	Share shape/"Make Better Seedbeds"	1910s	300–500
Grand Detour Plow Co. oval stickpin	Deere's first partner's later venture	1847–1919	50–100
Chrome-plated leaping deer tie clasp	On original card	1935	75–100
Gold-plated plow pin	John Deere on beam	1910–1940	50–100
Small flag "John Deere Plows"	Red, white & blue	late 1800s–early 1900s	100–300
"Inventor of the Steel Plow" button	White with gold Deere bust	1880s	50–100
"Up-To-Date" gold-rim KC branch pinback	"Saddles, Collars, Harness."	1896	250–350
Tiny white "Deere Bicycles" pin	Deer logo with large rack	1890s	300–500

Item	Remarks	Date	Value Range
Larger blue/white "Deere Bicycles" pin	"If you love me grin" wording	1890s	300–500
"New-Way Air-Cooled" engine (branch)	Celluloid pocket mirror	Unknown	100–300
Belt Buckles:			
Black & silver four-legged deer	Employee uniforms	1940s–1950s	200–600
Gold-plated two-legged deer	Dress design	1980s	20–40
Silver-plated 1936 logo	Small or large	1984	20–40
Large silver & green two-legged deer	Made by Wyoming prisoner	1990s	25–50
1876-style logo on half-moon shape	Gold-plated or silver	1983	20–40
Four generations of tractors (round)	Gold-plated or silver	1982	20–40
Four types of industrial equipment	Large gold-plated	1974	30–60
Deere bicycles trademark	Antique gold finish	1988	20–40
Waterloo Boy colored brass oval	"Kerosene tractors"	1990	20–40
The Furrow 100th anniversary	With black velvet pouch	1995	20–40
Men in field with plow 150th anniversary	Silver-plated	1987	20–40
Threshermen Collectors (Albert City, Ia.)	Pewter	1987	20–40
Pens and Pencils:			
Mechanical pencils (logos/equipment)	Dark green w/ pearl top	1950s–1960s	5–75
Bullet pencil (centennial)	Yellow	1937	25–50
Ballpoint pens (logos/equipment)	Green & yellow or pearlized body	1950s–1960s	5–75
Matches, Lighters, and Ashtrays:			
Two-cylinder Feature matchbooks	Tractor on matches	1938	20–50
Fertilizer matchbooks	From Pryor, Oklahoma	1952–1965	10–35
Chrome Zippo lighter	QFE logo & dealer imprint	1950s	50–90
Large green & yellow lighter	"Sparks New Earning Power"	Unknown	45–60
Gold Scripto with case	"125 Years"	1962	20–45
"Earthmoving-Logging" industrial lighter	Wellington black & gold	Unknown	100–200
White porcelain ashtray	QFE logo	1950s	25–40
Brass ashtray with red glass insert	Dealer imprint	1950s	25–50
Glass ashtray with green/yellow	Dealer imprint; no logo	1950s	25–40
Tape Measures:			
Celluloid with John Deere bust	Bright green, yellow & red	1930–1940	50–150
Celluloid with 1912 leaping deer logo	Bright green, yellow & red	1930–1940	50–150
Celluloid with 1950 QFE logo	Bright green, yellow & red	1950–1956	50–150
Celluloid with 1956 four-legged deer logo	Bright green & yellow	1956–1968	50–150
Deere & Webber trademark (large off-white)	With yellow, brown & blue	1880s–1910s	200–400
Aluminum John Deere Plow Co.	"World's Fair 1904"	1902–1905	200–400
Signs:			
John Deere Parts (green & yellow)	5x28 inches	1950	100–300
Veribrite "Farm Implements" (2x6 feet)	Black, yellow & red (Three-legged deer)	1910–1940	1,500
Deere Garage (green & yellow)	24 inches square (Four-legged logo)	1956–1968	100–200
Clocks and Watches:			
Square electric wall clock (17x14 inches)	Green & yellow (Four-legged logo)	1956–1968	500–1,000
Antique alarm clock with Model D on face	Reproduction	1990s	25–100
Pocket watches (jewel back)	Silver or gold (Four-legged logo)	1956–1968	80–150
Thermometers and Mirrors:			
"Good Luck" mirror/thermometer	Horseshoe, 1937 penny, QFE logo	1950–1956	50–100
"Long Line" mirror of styled Model A	With or without thermometer	1938–1947	50–150
"John Deere Implements" visor mirror	"Oil/Lube/Battery" areas	1920–1930s	80–250
"Many Brands" round desk mirror	Logos of 10 related companies	1900–1912	1,500–3,000

Item	Remarks	Date	Value Range
Wallets, Banks, and Coins:			
Titewad wallet	Deere bust/factory scene	1910–1940	25–75
Blacksmith mechanical bank	Cast-iron original	1976	150–300
Blacksmith mechanical bank	Reproduction/crude	1980s	25–50
Blacksmith mechanical bank	Colored plastic/New Orleans	1994	20–50
Blacksmith mechanical bank	Gold-colored plastic/New Orleans	1994	30–60
Green mailbox bank with yellow bird	Original/metal flag	1966	100–300
Kitchenware:			
Dual salt & pepper shakers	Clear/colored plastic	1950s	25–100
Bottle opener	Dealer imprint	1950s–1960s	5–50
Coffee mug	Ceramic	1980s	10–15
Coffee mug	Plastic	1980s	10–15
Paper cup	Green & yellow/logos	1950s–1960s	5–10

Chapter 3

Item	Remarks	Date	Value Range
Employee/Retiree Service Awards:			
Service pin/tie tack	Old style (oval w/ years)	1930–1970	30–70
Service pin/tie tack	Current style (round)	1975–1999	15–45
Men's or women's ring	Current style (round)	1975–1999	110–150
Women's necklace	Current style (round)	1975–1999	45–90
Money clip	Current style (round)	1975–1999	40–60
Cuff links	Current style (round)	1975–1999	35–75
Work Badges:			
Factory badge (with # underneath)	Colored background/Four-legged deer	1950s	90–200
Factory badge (with # in middle)	Round with color (no logo)	1940s–1950s	65–150
Mixed Car Warehouse badge	Silver octagon	Unknown	85–250
Factory badge (John Deere bust)	Name at top/number on bottom	Unknown	35–80
Spreader Works (Fire Dept.) shield	Four-legged leaping over log deer	1936	175–300
Related Companies:			
Sharples Cream Separator cello pinback	Woman with churn	1900–1910	40–60
Fort Smith Wagons pocket mirror	White with brown artwork	1905–1910	300–600
Moline Wagon trade card	Colorful wagon with horses	1870–1910	85–125
Van Brunt Drill ashtray	"Sample of material" (steel)	Unknown	10–30
Union Malleable horseshoe	Gold-plated (2 lb. 8 oz.)	Unknown	65–100
Syracuse Chilled Plow catalog	1897 catalog (red cover)	1897	35–80
Syracuse Chilled Plow trade cards	Colorful scenes	1890s	75–150
Syracuse Chilled Plow watch fob	Silver "Best in Earth"	1910s	65–125
Syracuse Chilled Plow watch fob	Gold-plated "Paris" design	1900	65–125
Success Spreader change tray	Colorful scene/lion head	1890–1910	80–150
Success Spreader globe pin holder	Lion head with globe art	1890–1910	150–200
Success Spreader watch fob	Wishbone with cross design	1890–1910	65–125
Success Spreader watch fob	Lion head with shield	1890–1910	45–125
Velie carriage tag	Brass with script lettering	1902–1919	35–85
Velie Motors Corp. medallion	Family crest (silver)	1916–1928	80–150
Velie/Deere letter opener	Brass	1900–1930	100–275
Velie car postcard	Black & white photograph	1908–1928	15–30
Velie brochure	Grand Canyon	1908–1928	35–85
Velie Vehicles pocket calendar	Leather/gold imprint	1900–1920	45–85
Velie Motor Vehicle hubcap	Gold-plated	1908–1916	50–90
Velie Motors Corp. hubcap	Aluminum	1916–1928	35–70
Velie radiator emblem	Letter "V" (blue & black)	1908–1928	80–140
John Deere Lanz pocketknife	Gold ornate with green logo	1956–1963	200–500
John Deere-Lanz keychain	Gold with green logo	1956–1963	45–100
John Deere-Lanz Swiss Army knife	Black with silver wording	1956–1963	55–125

Item	Remarks	Date	Value Range
John Deere-Lanz tape measure	Green & yellow with logo	1956–1963	65–125
Lanz ballpoint pen	Green & yellow (no logo)	1956–1963	20–50

Anniversary Items:

Item	Remarks	Date	Value Range
"Copper Pennies" wall hanging	Centennial designs (8-inch)	1937	200–600
Marble dual desk set (dealer)	"125 Years" w/ Four-legged logo	1962	100–300
Large pewter plate (foundry)	150th anniversary	1987	80–125
Gold-plated medallion	150th anniversary	1987	80–125
Marble/glass paperweight	150th anniversary	1987	40–90
Gold button cover set	150th anniversary	1987	50–100

Miscellaneous:

Item	Remarks	Date	Value Range
Calendar medallions	Gold-plated	1983–2000	15–30
Christmas ornaments	Pewter	1990s	35–125
Waterloo Boy "Good Luck" token	Two-sided coin; "Don't worry club"	1900–1920	65–125
"Shield of our Nation's Prosperity" tag	Two-sided cardboard (3 colors)	1880s	75–250
"Maltese Cross" hanging tag	Two-sided cardboard (3 colors)	1880s	75–250
Styled Model A shadow box	Green glass with cardboard scene	1938–1947	125–275
Walking plow replica (10-inch)	Cast-iron/nickel-plated (in box)	1912–1936	150–300
Walking plow replica (10-inch)	Aluminum/Chrome-plated (FFA)	1912–1936	80–150
Celluloid clothes brush (round)	John Deere bust/bright green & red	1930–1940s	300–600
Celluloid clothes brush (oblong)	1936 shield logo/bright green & red	1936-1940s	300–600
Formed brass deer coin bank	12 inches tall	Unknown	75–200
Brass log-leaping deer figurine	5 inches tall	Unknown	300–1,500
Album Songs With a Railroad Ring	"Power Train '66" promo	1966	15–35
Train replica of Burlington engine (red)	"Power Train '66" promo	1966	250–400
Letterholder (cast-iron/original or repro)	Belt around deer; "Moline, Ill. 1847"	1937–1990s	20–500

Chapter 4

Books, Magazines, and Catalogs:

Item	Remarks	Date	Value Range
John Deere's First 100 Years book	Neil Clark	1936	40–60
Children's book	Johnny Tractor and His Pals	1958	25/50/75
Children's book	Corny Cornpicker Finds a Home	1959	25/50/75
The Furrow magazine/U.S.	April, May, June issue	1897	65–75
The Furrow magazine/Canada	Special edition/patriotic issue	1943	30–60
The John Deere Magazine	Vol. 2, No. 1 (internal pub)	January 1919	35–80
Better Farming magazine		1909	45–60
Modern Farming magazine		1954–1964	30–45
Better Farm Implements magazine		1915	45–75
General Catalog	Dallas branch (No. 1)	1924	200–700
General Catalog	Kansas City branch (K)	1928	200–700
General Catalog	Deere & Co. (No. 31/32)	1911/1912	300–600
General Catalog	Kansas City branch (N)	1931	200–400
The Operation, Care, and Repair book	12th edition	1938	35–70
The Operation, Care, and Repair book	25th edition	1952	10–35

Brochures, Booklets, and Literature:

Item	Remarks	Date	Value Range
Deere & Mansur colorful tri-fold	Garden tools	1880s	100–200
Deere & Mansur colorful tri-fold	Moline Broadcast Seeder	1880s	80–150
Truth About Plow Shares booklet	30 pages	1915	45–90
The Science and Art of Plowing booklet	30 pages	1919	45–90
Waterloo Gasoline Traction Engine Co. lit	Froelich gasoline traction engine	1892	1,000–2,000
Model D literature	Oversized/yellow sky; 16 pages	1930	200–400
Model D literature	Black, yellow & orange; 28 pages	1935	100–150
Unstyled Model A, B, G literature	42 pages; color	1937	30–100
Styled Model A, B, G literature	Rust-colored cover; 42 pages	1938	30–100
Styled Model A literature	34 pages; w/ electric lights	1947	30–100

Item	Remarks	Date	Value Range
Model R Diesel literature	38 pages; color	1948–1954	30–100
Model MC crawler literature	16 pages; green & yellow	1947	30–70
Model 420 literature	20 pages; green & yellow	1955	30–60
Model 3020-4020 Standard literature	30 pages; color photo cover	1963	30–60
No. 7 combine (pull-type)	32 pages; b&w photo cover	1939	30–45
No. 45 combine (self-propelled)	38 pages; color cover	1956	20–45
No. 30 combine (pull-type)	30 pages; color cover	1958	15–30
How to Keep Your Farm Eqpt. in the Fight	67 pages; red, white & blue	ca. 1943	60–80
Hybrid Corn booklet	34 pages; bright yellow cover	1939	20–45
Soybeans for Profit booklet	32 pages; pale yellow cover	1936	20–45
Tractor cabs brochure	One color; Four-legged deer logo	1956–1968	20–45
Grove & Orchard tractors brochure	One color; Four-legged deer logo	1960–1968	50–150
Snowmobile literature	Color	1971–1982	20–30
Plow *Book of Verses* cartoons	10 pages; Gilpin Sulky	1887	100–300

Letterhead, Invoices, and Receipts:

Item	Remarks	Date	Value Range
Wagon Works envelope	Deere bust on front	1927	10–20
Deere & Webber envelope	Blue lithos of equipment	1910	10–30
Dealer envelope (Colorado)	Green & yellow lithos of equipment	1940s	40–90
Deere & Webber invoice	Sulky plow sale bill/Montana	1910	20–35
Print blocks (copper-type)	Logos, tractors, equipment	1930s–1950s	10–50

Pocket Ledgers and Calendars:

Item	Remarks	Date	Value Range
Pocket Companion	Red & gold cover	1883	100–300
Pocket Companion	Brown & green cover	1886	100–300
Pocket Companion	Red cover	1890	100–300
Pocket Companion	Blue trim on cover	1899	100–300
Pocket Companion	Purple cover	1903	100–300
Pocket Diary	Pale green cover	1878	100–300
Deere & Mansur Pocket Companion	Dark green with deer	1901	100–300
Pocket Companion	Yellow & blue cover	1905	100–300
Anniversary calendar	20x27 inches; Deere portrait	1937	250–800
Dealer calendar	"V for Victory" scene	1945	75–150

Postcards, Posters, Ads, and Annual Reports:

Item	Remarks	Date	Value Range
Deere & Co. plows trade card	Colorful pheasant hunt scene	1880s–1910s	100–300
Deere & Co. plows trade card	Colorful woman watering horse	1880s–1910s	100–300
Giant Moline wagon trade card	Colorful display of oversized wagon	1907	40–90
No. 127 corn picker poster	Colored	1954	50–100
No. 999 corn planter poster	Colored	1920	75–150
Model "70" Standard tractor poster	Colored	1954	50–100
"Farmer Gate" foldout card	Colored artwork	1880s	150–300
Advertisements	Black & white	1930s–1950s	2–10
Advertisements	Color	1930s–1950s	2–10
Annual report	Black & white	1920s–1930s	10–20
Annual report	Colorful	1940s–1950s	5–10

Chapter 5
Wrenches:

Item	Remarks	Date	Value Range
John Deere A196A	Lettering variations ("Deere")	1910–1930s	30–80
John Deere HZ836	Binders ("John Deere")	1920	50–100
John Deere 7321-C	Buggies ("Deere")	1903	125–250
Deere & Mansur B470	Disc cultivators & harrows	1900–1915	25–100
Deere & Mansur A522/A523	Two sizes; cylinder loaders	1900–1915	25–40
Dain #J81	"Ottumwa" or "Carrollton"	1890–1910	75–400
Dain #Z78	"Dain" mowers	1920s	10–50
Syracuse Chilled Plow Z2	"Syracuse"	1880–1920	10–50

Item	Remarks	Date	Value Range
Dain #Z78	"Dain" mowers	1920s	10–50
Syracuse Chilled Plow Z2	"Syracuse"	1880–1920	10–50
Syracuse Chilled Plow Z2	"John Deere"	1880–1920	250–300
Monkey wrench #HZ6758	All steel; binders & mowers	1920s	100–200
Monkey wrench #HZ5322 (10-inch)	Wooden handle; "John Deere"	1920s	200–300
Monkey wrench #HZ5322 (10-inch)	Wooden handle; "Deere Harvester"	1920s	200–300
Monkey wrench #HZ5322 (10-inch)	Wooden handle; "Deere & Co."	1920s	150–225
Van Brunt drills wrench	Original tool	1911	10–25
Van Brunt drills wrench	75th anniversary edition	1986	25–50
Miscellaneous Parts and Pieces:			
"Deere" cut-out toolbox (cast iron)	Three-sided design	Unknown	150–250
"Deere" cut-out toolbox (stamped steel)	Bottomless	Unknown	15–30
"John Deere" lettered toolbox (steel)	Bolted on beam of sulky plow	1910s	25–50
Hand #Y1656 (cast iron)	Planter demo display unit	1907	500–750
Foot pedal #B114H (cast iron)	John Deere binder	1923	15–50
Row marker H39M (cast iron)	Narrow track sower	1910s	100–175
"Deere" buggy step (cast iron)	From 4-passenger surrey	1900–1920	150–300
"Gilpin" cut-out toolbox (cast iron)	Sulky plow; 3-sided design	1875–1890	75–125
"Gilpin" cut-out footrest (cast iron)	Sulky plow	1875–1890	125–175
Seeder end L-1	Moline Broadcast Seeder	1885	25–100
Planter Lids:			
"John Deere. Moline, Ill." tin lid	No leaping deer logo (8-inch)	1910s	10–40
"John Deere. Moline, Ill." tin lid	Log-leaping deer logo (8-inch)	1910s	10–40
Deere & Mansur cast-iron lid Y1521	Deer & mountain scene; patent dates	1901–1907	30–75
Deere & Mansur cast-iron lid Y3025	Big-nosed deer; no mountain	1901–1907	50–125
Cast Iron Seats:			
"Deere & Co. Moline, Ill." cut-out	Sulky plows	1880s–1910s	100–250
Deere & Mansur ornate cut-out	11.5 inches round; Dropper seat	1880s–1910s	250–500
"Dain Co. Carrollton, Mo." slot	36 slot teardrop pattern	1880–1900	450–750
Syracuse Chilled Plow cut-out	"SCP Co." with pattern	1880–1910	75–300
Cans and Cartons:			
Oil can JD60H (red, blue, green, yellow)	Colored; John Deere/dealer name	1920s–1940s	75–120
Oil can with pump JD92	Yellow; Two-legged logo	post-1968	30–60
Oil can coin bank (green & yellow)	Two-cylinder tractors/Anniversary	1937	130–180
Oil can with pump JD93	Green; Four-legged logo	1956–1968	80–150
Small parts boxes	With QFE or Four-legged logo	1950–1968	5–25
Champion spark plugs carton	#AH830-R; QFE logo	1950–1956	45 each/300 carton
Fertilizer soil sampler bag	Pryor, OK; Four-legged logo	1956–1962	35–80
Fertilizer bulk bag (80 lb.)	Pryor, OK; "45 Nitrogen"	1956–1962	40–75
Fertilizer sample set dealer display	Plastic display with 6 vials	1956–1962	75–150

Chapter 6

Item	Remarks	Date	Value Range
1/16 Scale Tractors:			
Model A	Ertl's Precision Classics #1	1990/diecast	125–275
Model A w/ 290 cultivator	Ertl's Precision Classics #2	1991/diecast	325–475
Model 40 crawler (green)	Ertl	1954/diecast	225/350/650
Model 440 crawler (yellow)	Ertl	1959/diecast	200/300/600
Model 430 crawler (green)	Ertl	1997/diecast	45/65/75
Dain All-Wheel Drive	Joseph Murphy/Scale Models	1996/diecast	50–75
Waterloo Boy Model R (collector)	Ertl	1988/diecast	35–45
Model D (nickel driver/pulley)	Vindex	1930/cast iron	500–2,500
Stationary gas engine (on cart)	Vindex	1930/cast iron	350–950
Wagon or grain box (green/red)	Vindex	1930/cast iron	325–500

Item	Remarks	Date	Value Range
Van Brunt grain drill (red/yellow)	Vindex	1930/cast iron	700–3,000
Model A (open flywheel)	Ertl	1946/sand-cast aluminum	300–800
Model A (nickel driver)	Arcade	1940/cast iron	575–3,000
Model A	Ertl	1946/sand-cast aluminum	175–800
GP Wide Tread	Ertl	1995/diecast	25–35
Model G (Iowa FFA edition)	Ertl	1999/diecast	45–50
Model M (Series III collector)	Ertl	1986/diecast	25–35
Model 60 Orchard (collector)	Ertl	1993/diecast	25–35
Model 630	Ertl	1959/diecast	225–1000
Model 720 Hi-Crop (collector)	Ertl	1990/diecast	45–100
Model 3020 Diesel (wide front end)	Ertl	1964/diecast	125–275
Model 3020 Diesel (with ROPS)	Ertl	1969/diecast	175–500
Model 5020 Diesel	Ertl	1969/diecast	90–200
Model 7520 Four-Wheel Drive	Ertl	1972/diecast	300–800
Model 60	Ertl	1955/diecast	250–550
1/16 Scale Machinery:			
Loader	Eisele	1950/pressed steel	130–525
Plow (two-bottom)	Eska-Carter	1955/pressed steel	195–400
Model 494 planter (Four-row)	Ertl	1965/diecast	75–200
Model 12A combine (pull-type)	Eska-Carter	1952/pressed steel	100–425
Model 6600 combine (1/24 scale)	Ertl	1974/diecast	125–400
Model L manure spreader	Eska-Carter	1955/pressed steel	75–250
Disk (drag-type)	Eska-Carter	1950/pressed steel	75–250
Square baler (Model 14T)	Eska-Carter	1952/pressed steel	150–400
Model K manure spreader	Eska-Carter	1954/pressed steel	75–250
Disk harrow (4-gang)	Ertl	1950/diecast	95–250
Loader (Model 48)	Ertl	1962/diecast	75–150
Loader (Model 45)	Eska-Carter	1957/pressed steel	100–275
Wagon running gear	Arcade	1940/cast iron	175–2,000
Corn picker (Model 227)	Eska-Carter	1952/pressed steel	250–450
Wagon (flare box)	Eska-Carter	1952/pressed steel	100–200
Pedal Tractors:			
Model 20 pedal tractor	Ertl	1965/sand-cast aluminum	300–800
Model LGT pedal tractor	Ertl	1970/sand-cast aluminum	500–900
Miscellaneous:			
1907 Deere-Clark Type B car	Joseph Murphy/Scale Models	1992	30
1907 Deere-Clark Type C car	Joseph Murphy/Scale Models	1993	30
Snowmobile (Model 400)	Normatt	1972/plastic	75–250
Dain "Parts Express" Truck	Joseph Murphy/Scale Models	1989	10–25
Lanz Bulldog tractor (blue)	Rex	1959/plastic	400–700
Lanz combine (green)	Rex	1960/plastic	65–80
Stuffed deer (green & yellow)	B. J. Toy Company	1980s	350–2,000
"Master Farmer" board game	Unknown	1938/cardboard	50–250
NASCAR #23 car (1/18 scale)	Ertl	1996	75–125
NASCAR #97 car (1/64 scale)	Ertl	1997	30–50
Baseball bat (Louisville Slugger)	Unknown	Unknown	75–175
Children's book (Johnny Tractor)	Bell	1958/paper	25–50
Children's book (Corny Cornpicker)	Z&H	1959/paper	25–75
Goat wagon (reproduction)	Unknown	1980s	25–75
Reliance buggy	Joseph Murphy/Scale Models	1990/diecast	25
Farm wagon	Joseph Murphy/Scale Models	1989/diecast	20
Moline Wagon whistle	Unknown	1909/cardboard	100–300
Deere & Webber bicycle (man's)	Unknown	1890s	1,000–2,500
Bicycle trademark toy	Joseph Murphy/Scale Models	1993	10–25
Bicycle (green ladies three-speed)	John Deere	1972–1975	50–100
Bicycle (yellow girls banana-seat)	John Deere	1972–1975	200–400

Appendix B: Resources and References

Books

*The History of Old-Time Farm Implement Companies &
the Wrenches They Issued* (1999)
P. T. Rathbone
Route 1 Box 734
Marsing, Idaho 63639
(208) 896-4478

*International Directory of Model Farm Tractors &
Implements: Featuring John Deere, Volume I* (1993)
Raymond E. Crilley Sr. and Charles E. Burkholder
International Farm Models Publishing, Inc.
1881 Eagley Road
East Springfield, Pennsylvania 16411-9739

The Toy and the Real McCoy (1990)
Ralph C. Hughes
Deere & Company
Moline, Illinois 61265

John Deere Buggies and Wagons (1995)
Ralph C. Hughes

John Deere Tractors and Equipment (Volume I & II)
Don Macmillan & Russell Jones
American Society of Agricultural Engineers
2950 Niles Road
St. Joseph, Michigan 49085-9659

Classic John Deere Tractors (1994)
Randy Leffingwell
MBI Publishing Company
729 Prospect Ave, P.O. Box 1
Osceola, Wisconsin 54020
(800) 458-0454
www.motorbooks.com

John Deere Photographic History (1995)
Robert N. Pripps
MBI Publishing Company

Periodicals

Green Magazine
2652 Davey Road
Bee, Nebraska 68314
(402) 643-6269
www.greenmagazineonline.com

Two-Cylinder Magazine
P.O. Box 430
Grundy Center, Iowa 50638-0430
(319) 345-6060 or (888) 7TC-CLUB
www.two-cylinder.com

Farm Collector
1503 SW 42nd Street
Topeka, Kansas 66609-1265
(785) 274-4377
www.farmcollector.com

Antique Power
P.O. Box 500
Missouri City, Texas 77459
(800) 310-7047
www.antiquepower.com

The Replica
Ertl Company
Hwy 136
Dyersville, Iowa 52040
(319) 875-5613
www.ertltoys.com

Toy Farmer
7496 106th Avenue SE
LaMoure, North Dakota 58458-9404
(701) 883-5206 or (800) 533-8293
www.toyfarmer.com

Belt Pulley
20114 IL Route 16
Nokomis, Illinois 62075
(217) 594-7300
www.beltpulley.com

Toy Cars & Vehicles Magazine
Krause Publications
700 East State Street
Iola, Wisconsin 54990-0001
(715) 445-2214
www.krause.com/toys

Dick's Farm Toy Price Guide & Check List
24501 470th Avenue
Mapleton, Minnesota 56065
(507) 524-3275

Yesterday's Tractors Magazine
P.O. Box 160
Chimacum, Washington 98325
www.yesterdaystractors.com

Antique Trader Weekly
100 Bryant St.
Dubuque, Iowa 52004-1050
1-800-334-7165
www.collect.com

Places to Visit

John Deere Pavilion, Commons, Collector's Center, and Store
At the Riverfront (River Drive)
Moline, Illinois 61265
(309) 765-1000
www.johndeere.com

National Farm Toy Museum
1110 16th Avenue Ct. SE
Jct. Hwys. 20 & 136
Dyersville, Iowa 52040-2374
(319) 875-2727
www.dyersville.com

Auction Houses

Aumann Auctions
20114 IL Route 16
Nokomis, Illinois 62075
(217) 563-2523 or (888) AUCTN-4U
www.aumannauctions.com

Dennis Polk & Associates
Polk's *The Antique Tractor Magazine*
72435 SR 15
New Paris, Indiana 46553
219-831-3555 or 800-795-3501
www.dennispolk.com

Old Iron Auction
Norman O'Neal
3300 Lowell Lane
Ijamsville, Maryland 21754-9033
www.oldironauction.com

Clubs, Groups, and Organizations

Bleeding Green—The Official Book Site
"A community for John Deere collectors"
www.BleedingGreen.com

Two-Cylinder Club
P.O. Box 430
Grundy Center, Iowa 50638-0430
(319) 345-6060 or (888) 7TC-CLUB
www.two-cylinder.com

Toy Collector Club
1235 16th Ave. SE
Dyersville, Iowa 52040
(800) 452-3303
www.toycollectorclub.com

Antique Mechanics Club, Society, and Museum
Department of Biological and
    Agricultural Engineering
University of California
One Shields Avenue
Davis, California 95616
http://tractors.ucdavis.edu

Companies

Ertl Toys
The Ertl Company
Hwy. 136
Dyersville, Iowa 52040
(319) 875-5613
www.ertltoys.com

Spec-Cast
1235 16th Ave. SE
Dyersville, Iowa 52040
(800) 452-3303
www.speccast.com

Exocoin
Coins, Collectibles, & Exonumia
P.O. Box 720900
Oklahoma City, Oklahoma 73172
(800) 860-7558
www.exocoin.com

*Maloney's Online Antiques & Collectibles
Resource Directory*
David Maloney, Jr.
PO Box 2049
Frederick, MD 21702-1049
www.maloneysonline.com

Fastrac
An Antique Tractor Support Group &
Information Site
Dave Haynes, Adept Resources
P.O. Box 2297
Elkhart, Indiana 46515
www.adeptr.com

Sites on the World Wide Web

Antique Tractor Internet Service
"The World's Oldest Website for Antique Tractors"
Spencer Yost
www.atis.net

Powertown USA
Powertown Corporation
P.O. Box 707
Janesville, Wisconsin 53547-0707
(800) 274-5468
www.powertownusa.com

Antique Tractors
Yesterday's Tractors Magazine
P.O. Box 160
Chimacum, Washington 98325
www.antiquetractors.com

Dan's Tractor Restoration
8933 Lower Rocky River Road
Concord, North Carolina 28025
(704) 455-9344
www.restorum.com

INDEX